St.Peter's

EPISCOPAL CHURCH

OXFORD, MISSISSIPPI

A HISTORY 1851-2011

BY BRENDA J. WEST

FIRST EDITION   First printing, 2011
                          Second printing, 2012
                          Third printing, 2019

ISBN: 978-1-949455-07-6

For additional copies or bulk discounts, contact St. Peter's Episcopal Church at 113 South 9th Street Oxford, MS 38655 • Tel: (662) 234-1269
administrator@stpetersoxford.org • http://www.stpetersoxford.org

The Episcopal Diocese of Mississippi

Post Office Box 23107
Jackson, Mississippi 39225-3107

John Maury Allin
Episcopal Diocesan House
118 North Congress Street
Jackson, Mississippi 39201-2604

Toll-free: 866-550-0872
Telephone: (601) 948-5954
Facsimile: (601) 354-3401
Electronic Mail: info@dioms.org
Website: www.dioms.org

The Bishop
The Rt. Rev. Duncan M. Gray III, D.D.
Diocesan

The Diocesan Staff
The Rev. Canon David H. Johnson
Canon to the Ordinary

Canon Kathryn Weathersby McCormick
Canon for Administration and Finance

The Rev. Annie C. Elliott
Coordinator for Youth Ministries

Ms. Liley P. Gilbert
Bookkeeper

Mr. Edgar Glover
Sexton

Mrs. Peggy C. Jones
Assistant to the Bishop

The Rev. Scott Lenoir
Mississippi Episcopalian Editor

Ms. V. A. Patterson
Archivist

Ms. Suzanne Phillips
Assistant to the Canons

March 18, 2011

St. Peter's Church is a remarkable place. Over 150 years ago a community of faith gathered together to address the spiritual and intellectual needs of the newly established university in Oxford. Their choice of the Rev. Dr. F.A.P. Barnard, the University's first chancellor, to be their first rector, set a tone for the relationship between St. Peter's and Ole Miss that has greatly influenced both through the years.

When St. Peter's has been most faithful to its calling it has sought to minister to the deepest needs of the human mind, body and spirit. It has faced courageously the enormous cultural changes that have taken place over 150 years and has been a community where thoughtful, prayerful discernment of God's purposes for its common life has become the norm.

It has been a haven for those seeking a deeper relationship with God in the person of Jesus Christ through the power of the Holy Spirit. Saint and sinner, artist and agnostic, faithful and fretful have all found a home in a community that gathers around a common altar to offer their broken lives in service to the Risen Lord.

May the Lord, who in ages past called God's people to lives of witness and service, be forever the cornerstone of this special community.

Faithfully,

The Rt. Rev. Duncan M. Gray, III
Ninth Bishop of the
Episcopal Diocese of Mississippi

Preface

When St. Peter's celebrated its Centennial Anniversary in 1951, The Rev. William Asger wrote a history of the church's first 100 years. When St. Peter's celebrated its 125th Anniversary in 1976, Dr. John Crews, Professor of English at the University of Mississippi, continued Asger's work and wrote a history of the church's first 125 years, *A Goodly Heritage*. Continuing this tradition of updating St. Peter's history as part of the church's anniversary celebrations, I have updated the writings of Asger and Crews as part of St. Peter's 150th anniversary. We have actually recognized two 150th anniversaries: the Sesquicentennial Celebration of 2001, when we celebrated the establishment of the church, and the 150th Celebration of 2010-2011, when we celebrated the birthday of the actual building – the bricks and mortar that continue to provide our sacred worship space, the oldest religious structure in Oxford. I am grateful to Asger and Crews for documenting our rich history with earlier anniversary editions.

John Crews was the first to read this manuscript and encourage me to strike out with "my own words." I still used, with his blessings, much of his earlier research from "A Goodly Heritage." So many friends from St. Peter's helped to make this manuscript much richer: Charles Reagan Wilson, my advisor throughout this process, patiently read and reread copy and offered scholarly advice along the way; Charles Dollar asked important questions that sent me off on additional research; Mary Ann Reed Bowen counted every ellipsis and reminded me of forgotten grammatical rules; Allan Alexander worked to eliminate the use of passive tense and offered many excellent suggestions; Michael Dean, Jean Kiger and Debra Young all shared their knowledge of church history and eye for detail; and Oxford historian Jack Lamar Mayfield provided important details on local history. My thanks go also to other advance copy readers: Gloria Kellum, Lucy Turnbull, Sara Davidson, Michael de L. Landon, and son-in-law, Doug Harper. Calls of encouragement from the two Bishops Gray reassured me of the importance of documenting our rich heritage and kept me focused. The Rev. Taylor Moore has been an enthusiastic supporter for this documentation from the beginning, and Jennifer West, St. Peter's Parish Administrator, always provided smiling assistance when asked.

Parishioner and publisher Neil White has been on board from the beginning and gave me confidence in this project from the first time we met. The combined talents and support everyone has given to this project certainly exemplifies the love we all share for St. Peter's.

And, loving appreciation to Bill West for not complaining when I disappeared for hours while working on this project and for those many meals he prepared when I lost track of time.

My thanks to David Sansing for encouraging me to not be restricted by any scholarly format for endnotes, but to present the sources I used in a manner that, hopefully, will make it easier for the reader to enjoy the story of our church and to have access to additional resources if desired. Web addresses were correct at the time of this publication.

It is with love for this church that embraced my family from the first time we walked through these historic doors, the church where our family was confirmed, where our children were married, where our grandchildren were baptized, that I offer *St. Peter's Episcopal Church: A History 1851-2011*. May this third edition of our history continue to bestow on us all "the love of Christ which transforms lives."

Brenda Jones West
Senior Warden, 1995-1997

Contents

Prayer for St. Peter's

ALMIGHTY God who did establish Thy Church to show forth Thy Truth and Love unto all nations; send anew Thy Holy Spirit upon St. Peter's. Inspire our praises and receive the prayers of all who worship Thee through His church. Be gracious unto Thy servants and grant that every member in his vocation and ministry may work and pray and give for the spread of Thy Kingdom. Keep us mindful and thankful for all those who have gone before us and served here in this place. Grant that we might continue that witness for Christ and His church in this city, diocese and nation, and direct us that we may be a community of prayer, of healing, and of service to the glory of Thy Holy Name. All this we ask in the name of Jesus Christ, our Lord.

Amen.

Source unknown

St. Peter's Mission

"To share the love of Christ which transforms lives."

Adopted 1995

1

Our Firm Foundation
1840-1860

"The history of the Episcopal Church in Oxford provides a chapter in the cultural history of the South. It begins in the 1840s, a time of migration of people from the East to this section of the country, and continues on to include the slavery controversy, secession, Civil War, Reconstruction, the Southern artistic renaissance of the 20th Century, the civil rights struggle of the 1960s and its aftermath. Members of St. Peter's congregation played conspicuous roles in these events. Founded by slaveholders more than 150 years ago, St. Peter's is a parish that became dedicated to racial reconciliation efforts and outreach programs to the Oxford community." So began John Crews' 1976 history of St. Peter's, *A Goodly Heritage*.

The first Episcopal services in Oxford were held in 1840, the year The Reverend Andrew Matthews, Episcopal missionary for North Mississippi living in Hernando, was making a tour of territory recently held by the Chickasaw Nation. The village of Oxford, settled in 1837, had been incorporated one year after Lafayette County was formed in 1836.

Matthews was the father of the church in the northern part of the state. He founded two Episcopal churches in Desoto County, one in Hernando and a second at Wakefield, started the church at Grenada and held services for the Episcopal flock in Oxford. He supported himself by his farming, not by his missionary activity. On December 10, 1840, he wrote of his visits to Oxford, noting an increase in the number of Episcopalians from one on his first trip to eight on later ones:

"I visited Oxford, Lafayette County, in the month of September, officiated twice, and baptized two children. There I found some Episcopal families, one of whom is about to remove to this place in consequence of my settling here. On my first visit to this new village, I found but one Episcopalian. I officiated twice on the following Sunday, more I presume for a congregation of astonished spectators than humble worshippers."

On his next visit, Matthews mentions the organization of a church in Oxford and his acceptance of the call to serve the people of the new church. He concludes his account with:

"I commenced my duties on the Seventh Sunday after Trinity. The service has been regularly kept since that time. I have administered Holy Communion twice, the number that partook each time being twelve; eight of who were Episcopalians. I think, through the grace of God, we have the prospect of an increase."

Along with Matthews, clergy from nearby towns, possibly from St. John's in Pontotoc, Grace Church in Okolona, or Christ Church in Holly Springs, served the congregation in the 1840s. The Rt. Rev. James Hervey Otey, provisional Bishop of Mississippi whose Episcopal authority at one time extended from Florida to Arkansas, visited Oxford on Sunday, October 22, 1848. The bishop, perceiving the important role the congregation could play in relation to the newly established University of Mississippi, wrote in his journal:

"At Oxford, Lafayette County, I read Morning Prayer in the Presbyterian Church, baptized three children and preached. This place being in the close neighborhood of the University of Mississippi, which has recently commenced operations, and to which the young from various parts of the state may be expected to resort, should receive immediate attention from the church. An active and efficient missionary ought now to be on the ground sowing the precious seed of God's truth, and laboring diligently for the plenteous harvest, which sooner or later never fails to reward the work of faith and labor of love."

The University of Mississippi, 1848

In 1850, just months after being consecrated as the 1st Bishop of Mississippi on February 24, The Right Reverend William Mercer Green arrived on the scene and laid the groundwork for the establishment of St. Peter's Episcopal Church. Bishop Green spoke of efforts to build a church here and, like provisional Bishop Otey, cited its importance to the university. About his visit here on November 22, 1850, the newly consecrated Bishop Green wrote:

"I passed over to Oxford. The following day was occupied in visiting several families of the place, supposed to be friendly to the Church. I was pleased to meet here with The Rev. Dr. Sparrow of Alexandria (Virginia) Seminary..... It was no little gratification to me, as an adopted Mississippian, to find the University of the State furnished with so able a Faculty and provided with so many facilities for a thorough and liberal education. In the village and neighborhood of Oxford, I found several individuals and families desirous of enjoying our services and willing to do what they could towards procuring them. They even spoke of attempting to build a church, a liberal individual (Col. Jno. D. Martin) of Holly Springs having presented a suitable lot for that purpose...."

"President Longstreet, with a liberality becoming his station and character, ex-

pressed his gratification at hearing that it was in contemplation to add another place of worship to those already within reach of the University.... No feature in the regimen of the University impressed me more favorably... than the permission allowed to each student to worship God in such place and in such way on the Sabbath as either his own preference or the will of his parents might select. On Sunday, the 24th, I preached in the morning in the Presbyterian Church, politely tendered for the purpose; and Dr. Sparrow in the afternoon."*

*Augustus B. Longstreet, President of the University of Mississippi, 1849-1856, was also a Methodist minister, author, judge, and politician.

Bishop William Mercer Green, 1st Bishop of the Diocese
of Mississippi, 1849-1887

In response to the desire to establish a church here, Bishop Green scheduled a spring visit to Oxford the next year for the purpose of forming an Episcopal congregation. He and The Rev. Mr. Lynd of Holly Springs conducted services on May 11, 1851, to a full house of Episcopalians and curious onlookers. Bishop Green announced at that service that there would be an organizational meeting the next afternoon, May 12th, at the Lafayette County Courthouse.

In his account of the organizational meeting, the Bishop again takes notice of the proximity of the University of Mississippi and the church's important role there, ministering to Episcopalians and non-Episcopalians. He refers to the congregation's offer of $300 to a clergyman who could hold services twice a month, and mentions the continuing desire of Oxford Episcopalians to erect a church. Details from his journal reveal enthusiastic support for an Episcopal presence in this young town:

"May 10, 1851, I passed over to Oxford, the last point which I aimed to reach in my present visitation. This place properly belongs to my autumnal visitation, but from the position in which I left matters there on my former visit in November, I deemed another expedient at the present time.

Sunday May 11, preached both in the forenoon and at night in the Presbyterian Church, assisted in the services by The Rev. Mr. Lynd. The Church was filled on both occasions; and I was glad to see a number of Prayer-Books in use, as well as to notice the manifest interest excited by our services in many who had seldom, if ever, witnessed them before. None were confirmed; but I heard of three or four who would probably present themselves as candidates for that Apostolic rite at my next visit in November. At the close of the evening services, I gave notice of an intended meeting of friends and members of the church, to be held the next afternoon in the Courthouse; and invited all interested to attend."

Bishop Green's journal entry from that Monday, May 12, again reveals his enthusiasm for this new congregation, along with his concern that his support could be construed as "undue partiality" to the church in Oxford. He described those in attendance at the organizational meeting as *"between twenty and thirty of the most intelligent and respectable citizens of the town and vicinity...."* Prof. John Millington, L.L.D., opened the meeting in the courthouse and the congregation was duly organized as "St. Peter's Church." A Vestry and Wardens were elected in canonical form. Bishop Green baptized three children at the end of the meeting.

"Nor should I be regarded as showing my undue partiality to this undertaking when I commend it, as I now do, to the special attention of every portion of the Diocese. At this place is the University of the State ... there are now between one and two hundred students in the various Departments, and the number is increasing. Among them are to be found some of the sons of the Church, baptized at her altar, and trained in their boyhood in her Evangelical principles. To take due care of such, to preserve them from the temptations of college life, and to keep them in the way in which they have been trained, is certainly the duty of that church to which they look to as a nursing mother. Nor is it less our duty to present our ministrations in as favorable a light as possible before those youths who are not of our flock, but who nevertheless may be won by her solemn worship and her Scriptural teachings to give their hearts to God. It is upon these grounds that I now bespeak the favorable regards of the Diocese generally in the attempt to erect a Church at that place, and to provide it with a suitable Minister. Small as their number is, they liberally offer three hundred dollars toward the support of a clergyman, who will officiate for them on two Sundays in the month. If they should attempt soon to erect a Church, I trust that, for the reasons given above, every part of the Diocese will contribute something toward the undertaking."

Before the Bishop returned home on May 13, he asked the newly elected Vestry to meet and pass a resolution requesting admission into union with the other Congregations of the diocese. St. Peter's Church was officially organized.

The parish register identifies the three children baptized that day in the courthouse as William Johnson Belcher and Eleazer Crabtree Belcher, infant sons of Edward R. and E.A. Belcher, and Lucius Thornwell Pegues, infant son of Alexander H. and Rebecca Pegues. The Pegues came to the area around 1836 and were among the largest landowners in the county. Alexander Pegues is listed as junior warden at the founding meeting of St. Peter's. The Pegues family continued to figure prominently in the life of the church. The stained glass window, "Blessed are the pure in heart," is a memorial to Samuel, also son of Alexander and Rebecca Pegues. Another window, "Christ as the Good Shepherd," is in memory of another branch of this prominent family.

Baptisms

William Johnson) Infant son of Edward R
Elezar Crabtree) and E. A. Belcher

Lucius Thornwell Infant Son of Alexander
H. Pegues and R. A. Pegues his wife.
The above were Baptized in the Court House
of Oxford on the afternoon of May 12th 1851
by Bishop Green, immediately after the
organization of Saint Peters Church.

Teste

John Millington
Senr. Church Warden.

Among those "intelligent and respectable citizens" that the bishop mentioned was John Millington, the first senior warden at St. Peter's. Bringing with him his library and scientific instruments, Millington was one of the University's four original faculty members in 1848. He had come to the University at the age of 69 as the first professor of natural sciences from the College of William and Mary where he had been chairman of the department of chemistry, natural philosophy, and engineering. His earlier career was spent in England, where he had been an associate with famed scientists Michael Faraday, Sir Humphrey Davy, and William Herschel. Millington wrote the first American textbook on civil engineering, published in 1839. An excerpt from the William and Mary College Quarterly Historical Magazine (January 1923) describes him as being "an earnest adherent, persistent in faith, zealous in practice, unobtrusive and undemonstrative in expression. His religion accorded with his whole life, which was spent in fruitful performance, not in ostentatious profession. In keeping with these dispositions, he was an active participant in the establishment of the Episcopal Church at Oxford, Mississippi."

John Millington, 1st Senior Warden at St. Peter's 1851

The period 1851 to 1861 represents a critical time in St. Peter's history, not only for Episcopalians, but for the entire Oxford community. With the establishment of the congregation in 1851, the determination to find a full-time rector, and the celebration of the first service in the new church in 1860, St. Peter's assumed a leadership role in the community, one that continues today.

The Rev. Chauncey Colton, who served as both rector of St. Thomas Hall, a Military Academy in Holly Springs, and associate rector at Christ Church, Holly Springs, wrote in his 1852 report to the Diocese:

"Since its organization in May 1851, this Parish has enjoyed no regular services since February last. Since that time I have visited it monthly, officiating twice on each visit, and returning on Sunday night to my duties at St. Thomas Hall, Holly Springs."

Rebecca Pegues' July 8, 1853, journal entry exemplifies the determination of local citizens to have an Episcopal church in Oxford:

"I have been thinking all the morning about our prospects as regards the church – getting an Episcopal Church built and a minister – I have resolved in my own mind to promise to pay annually out of my private means 25 dollars to a minister and 25 dollars toward building the church from 1st of Jan 1853 until it is finished and furnished."

The Rev. T.B. Lawson took charge of St. Peter's on April 1, 1854, and his summary of parish activity for that year reported eight families and $2000 contributed towards building a church. He was preaching in Oxford once a month at the Presbyterian Church. He apparently lived quite a distance from Oxford and also served churches in Pontotoc and Okolona. Bishop Green confirmed Jacob Thompson, Alexander Hamilton Pegues, John Thompson, and Eloise Pomeroy on his December 10, 1854, visit. Shortly thereafter in 1855, the church secured a full time minister in the person of The Rev. Prof. Frederick Augustus Porter Barnard, who had served the church as Deacon until his ordination on December 2, 1855. Prof. E.W. Hilgard of the University faculty gave this account of Barnard's ordination:

"The good people of Oxford had up to that time been almost unacquainted with the Episcopal service; they were Methodists, Baptists, and Presbyterians of various shades of opinion and the few Episcopalians then resident among them were looked upon as kind of mild heretics, excusable only because they comprehended such highly respected people as Jacob Thompson and the Pegues families. But the very name of priest, when mentioned in connection with the impending ordination, seemed to give rise to a kind of holy horror, manifested in whispered conversations on the street corners and elsewhere; and the momentous question whether a true Protestant could conscientiously sanction by his presence such a proceeding was decided in the affirmative by the influence of intense female curiosity.... The little Baptist church occupied for the occasion was thronged; but the general sentiment seemed to be that the whole proceeding savored of popery, and Barnard was for a time regarded with less favor than ever."

In the 1855 report of the parish, The Rev. Lawson expressed his confidence that the "zealous and faithful" parish, under the leadership of The Rev. Prof. Barnard, would be successful in their determination to build a church. The church building was indeed finished in 1860, and Barnard delivered the first sermon in the new church on Easter Sunday, April 8, 1860. In his sermon, Barnard congratulated the congregation with these words:

"[T]hat you are, at length gathered together in this beautiful, though unpretending edifice reared by yourselves to the worship of God. Hitherto, like the Israelites in their captivity, you have had neither temple nor altar and in…your privation and desolation you have suffered as they suffered, when by the rivers of Babylon, they sat down and wept."

Barnard's wife, Margaret McMurray Barnard, worked with biographer John Fulton, who in1896, completed *Memoirs of Frederick A. P. Barnard, 10th President of Columbia College in the City of New York*. Barnard had died in 1889 in New York, and sadly, Mrs. Barnard died in 1891 before the memoirs were published. Fulton continued working with the material she had provided, and relayed Barnard's interesting account of their move from Alabama to Oxford, Mississippi:

"There were many difficulties attending our removal to Oxford. We had to drive there, of course, and on the very evening before we were to start, a valuable horse that I had had for several years took suddenly ill and died. My books and furniture had to be sent by a very roundabout way, first down the river 400 miles to Mobile, thence by sea 200 miles to New Orleans, thence up the Mississippi 500 hundred miles to Memphis, and then sixty miles by wagon to Oxford.…"

Jacob Thompson was another one of the highly respected parishioners at Barnard's ordination. Bishop Green had baptized and confirmed his wife, Catherine Jones Thompson, on November 23, 1851, three years before Thompson's confirmation. Thompson had served in Congress from 1839 until 1851, then practiced law and took care of his vast farming operations. He was Chairman of the Board of Trustees of the University of Mississippi when, in 1854, Barnard reluctantly left the University of Alabama and agreed to serve as Chair of Mathematics and Natural Philosophy at the University of Mississippi. The Southern politician and the Yale-educated Rector from Massachusetts remained friends throughout their time together at St. Peter's.

Frederick A.P. Barnard, Rector: 1855-1861
Chancellor of The University of Mississippi: 1856-1861

Jacob Thompson: 1810-1885

JOURNAL

OF THE

THIRTY-FIFTH ANNUAL CONVENTION

OF THE

Protestant Episcopal Church,

IN THE

DIOCESE OF MISSISSIPPI.

HELD IN CHRIST CHURCH, HOLLY SPRINGS,
April 25, 26 and 27, 1861.

JACKSON:
MISSISSIPPIAN BOOK AND JOB OFFICE.

1861.

2
The Civil War Takes Its Toll
1861-1865

The Diocese's Thirty-Fifth Annual Convention was held at Christ Church in Holly Springs in April 1861.

Bishop Green addressed those present with these words:

"DEAR BRETHREN:

"*An eventful year has passed over us since we last took counsel together. Our political sky has for some time been overcast by clouds of the most threatening aspect; but a strong and merciful arm has thus far either suspended or turned aside their bolts. The revolution which has been forced upon us has been effected in a manner no less wonderful than grateful to every heart. What may yet be in reserve for us, we cannot tell. In the hands of the wise and merciful God of Nations, we must leave our country, with the earnest supplications of Christian hearts, and the firm resolves of patriots trusting in the righteousness of their cause.*

"*But whilst the State is thus passing through the fires of a painful revolution, how thankful should we be that the Church is at peace; and that although our political relations towards our brethren with whom we have hitherto so lovingly associated have been severed, no change of name, of government, or national interest, will be able to lessen our affection for them as fellow-members with us of the One, Holy, and Apostolic Communion which is in Christ Our Lord. If a separate and independent Ecclesiastical organization shall be demanded by the change in our political relations, it will exhibit to the world a division without dissension, a separation without injury to the respective parts, a parting of brothers amid tears of affection, and with a mutual commending of each other to God."*

Bishop Green closed the convention with this plea:

"I trust that no son of the Church will withhold himself or his from any call which his country can make upon him. But, beloved brethren, whilst we keenly feel the wrongs which have driven us to this separation, and are as firmly resolved, with God's help, to maintain our position, let us not, in the fervor of our patriotism, forget that we are Christian men, and yield to feelings of hatred and revenge more than a true love of country calls for at our hands. A manly and persistent defense of our rights is in no way incompatible with a just and charitable appreciation of those who seek to wrong us, or even with fervent prayer that an Almighty God may lead them to a better mind, and take from them their evil purposes rather than their lives. But turning from those whom I am so loath to call our enemies, let me remind you of Him in whose hands are the fates of nations as well as of individuals, and from whom alone come both victory and defeat. If ever there was a time when prayer should be fervent and unceasing, that time is the present, when we are threatened with the horrors of a fratricidal war, when friends and neighbors, and kindred, and brothers seem about to mingle in bloody strife. But dreadful as is the spirit of this unnatural struggle, it may yet be driven out by prayer and fasting. Let us then, both Clergy and Laity, besiege the throne of grace with our supplications for our country, her rulers, her legislators, and all who have gone forth in her defense. Let us suppress all bitterness and wrath towards others and all envying and jealousies among ourselves. Let us, in every way, uphold the law and seek to promote order. So shall we best serve the State, and draw down upon our institutions and people the blessing of Him "without whom nothing is strong, nothing is holy."

Barnard's annual report from St. Peter's parish register was recorded in the 1861 Convention's publication as:
• Families, number of   13
• Children, White,   2
• Communicants—Former number, White,   20
• Communicants—Added,   4
• Removed,   1

The appendix to the convention's proceedings contains the Bishop's journal, written a few days before the convention, in which he recognizes the need for a full time minister at St. Peter's:

"Saturday and Sunday, 13th and 14th, were spent in Oxford. On Sunday, I preached in their new and beautiful Church, which, with the exception of a debt upon it, though not to any great amount, is ready for Consecration. This congregation is much in need of a Minister who can give himself without restraint to parochial labor. The gratuitous services of President Barnard, have for several years served to keep the flock together; but it cannot be expected that he should continue them much longer, in addition to the many and arduous duties devolved upon him by the University."

Even though Barnard had come to Mississippi from Alabama, his New England background was enough to create mistrust among a few faculty members who were eager to see him leave the University. These feelings were heightened when Barnard expelled two students who assaulted his female slave in 1859. That Barnard would dismiss a white student on the basis of "negro testimony" gave ammunition to those wanting Barnard to give up his position. The effort failed, however, and Barnard's staunchest supporters, in addition to Jacob Thompson, were Bishop Green and Prof. E.W. Hilgard. Bishop Green had talked to Barnard about becoming the first president of The University of the South, which would be opening soon at Sewanee. Shortly after the April 1861 meeting in Holly Springs, Thompson and Barnard served as official delegates at the Montgomery, Alabama meeting when the Protestant Episcopal Church in the Confederate States was formed. Alexander Pegues of this congregation was an alternate delegate to the convention.

Decisions made by Bishops, Clergy, and Laymen at this critical time in our church history rested on the conception that the Holy Catholic Church was made up of autonomous national churches. Not until after the war did Bishop Green *"show the world that the Holy Catholic Church of Christ, however separated by political boundaries, is still one."*

Near the end of his tenure at the University and St. Peter's, Barnard spoke again of suffering, not of the Israelites in their captivity as he had done in his first sermon, but of another type of suffering, this time from the war dividing the country.

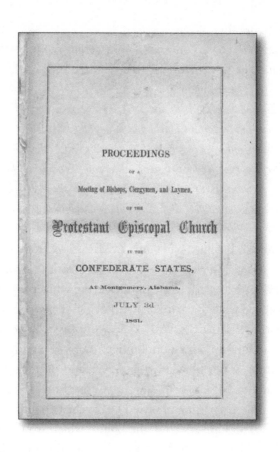

PROCEEDINGS

OF A

Meeting of Bishops, Clergymen, and Laymen,

OF THE

Protestant Episcopal Church

IN THE

CONFEDERATE STATES,

At Montgomery, Alabama.

JULY 3d

1861.

July 1861

In a sermon delivered at Oxford on June 13, 1861, his closing words were these: *"Let me, in conclusion, recall your attention to the lesson which it has been my object this evening to inculcate. If God has visited us with affliction, let us remember that we have shown ourselves but parsimoniously grateful for His abundant mercies. If He threatens to bring us low, let us bear in mind that the loftiness of our pride has merited His just displeasure. Let us therefore seek His face with deep contrition and humility of heart, humbly beseeching Him to make our present trials the means of reclaiming us to Him, and of making us, as individuals and as a people, more faithful in our duty than we have ever yet been, or than we ever would have been, had we not been afflicted. And, in the words of our most worthy and well-beloved Bishop and Father in God, let us entreat Him, in His infinite wisdom and power, so to overrule events, and so to dispose the hearts of all engaged in this painful struggle, that it may soon end in peace and brotherly love, and lead not only to the safety, honor, and welfare of our Confederate States, but to the good of all His people and the glory of His great Name, through Jesus Christ our Lord."*

After Barnard left Oxford in 1861, the Church was closed until the end of the Civil War. The Bishop conducted the only services during his annual visitation. In 1862, Mr. T.E.B. Pegues represented St. Peter's at the Annual Council of the Parish and was chosen Lay Deputy to the General Council which met in November of that year in Augusta, Georgia. There were no reports from St. Peter's until 1865, when Bishop Green visited, baptizing six and confirming nine. According to Diocesan Journal entries compiled by Miss Frances Walthall, there was no minister in charge. At war's end, Bishop Green summarized the depressed state of things as follows:

"The reduced number of our clergy, the destruction of some of our churches, the robbery and defacement of others, the general impoverishment of our people, and the total ruin of many, joined to the complicated claims, the embittered feelings, and the disregard of moral obligation…have thrown our church several years back."

Nowhere is the sad state of financial affairs impacting St. Peter's and the Diocese of Mississippi more evident than in the Proceedings of the 1862 General Council. The reports show that Mississippi contributed $1 to the Foreign Mission fund and $1 to the Domestic Mission fund. An interesting comparison may be made to the Diocese of South Carolina that gave $1416 to the foreign missions and $882 to missions at home.

Mrs. Alexander (Rebecca) Pegues, a devout Episcopalian, kept a diary which revealed her impression of the war years. On May 10, 1860, she wrote, *"I have been interested in reading the proceedings of the Charleston Convention. Affairs seem to have reached somewhat of a crisis between the North and the South."* Her entries are dated sometimes weekly, sometimes monthly, and vividly describe her thoughts and daily activities during the war. When the invading army reached Holly Springs and was closer to "Orange Hill" her plantation home, she took her family to Alabama. Before she left, she described the exodus of many citizens: *"It was discouraging to see so many of them running off – fearful of arrest – deserting their homes, and leaving the women at the mercy of the invaders."*

When she returned to Oxford two years later, she wrote, *"Then we went to Oxford and rented a house with three rooms. We had no store rooms, no pantry, no dining room nor room for the boys. We had but little furniture left."* October 31, 1865.

Mrs. Rebecca Pegues 1816-1889

Another important historical contribution was her "Sketch of St. Peter's Parish" that she carefully and diligently recorded. A copy of this handwritten document, which covers 1851-1871, is preserved in St. Peter's archives. As noted in Mrs. Pegues' beautiful hand, the sketch contains a "Record of events concerning St. Peter's Church, Oxford, culled from the Diocesan Journals, and from the Bishop's addresses therein."

Forty years after the war, a Prayer Book was returned to St. Peter's with the following inscription:

"This book was brought to the writer at Oxford, Mississippi, August 20, 1864, by his colored servant boy while buildings were being burned and houses and stores

were being looted by Federal troops. After being in his possession 40 years and it being the only relic he has of the war, he is desirous of returning it to the owner if he or she can be found, if not he presents it to the Church at Oxford, Mississippi, as a souvenir of the great war, by one who so far as lay in his power protected women and children and prevented the wanton destruction of private property." Signed: Edward H. Couse. Ex. Adjt. 9th Minn., Vol. Infantry.

This Prayer Book was returned to the church in February 1905, and remains with other historical papers in a security box at First National Bank, Oxford.

The church was not damaged during the war, although Federal troops burned the courthouse just three blocks away and desecrated Christ Church in nearby Holly Springs. Sansing writes of Barnard's earlier friendship with General Sherman when Sherman was president of Louisiana Seminary in Baton Rouge (later LSU), and the General's friendship with Barnard's younger brother, John, former Commander of West Point. Sansing cites a July 28, 1863, letter found in the Columbia Library from Sherman to Barnard: "When I rode through the grounds of the college, I thought of you and asked where you lived." When he was shown the observatory, Sansing writes, Sherman replied that he could see Barnard's hand in the building. Perhaps he had similar thoughts when he saw the beautiful church where Barnard served as Rector.

John Sobotka's *History of Lafayette County*, describes the picture above as "Ruins of Oxford, Miss., 1864," so named by Oxford resident, Capt. William Neill. Jack Mayfield, local historian, identifies the columned building on the left as the old Cumberland Presbyterian Church on South Lamar. Mayfield says the outside of the church was changed from Greek Revival to Gothic in the early 1880s, and that in the 1930's, the DAR Chapter in Oxford verified that this was Oxford. Mayfield suggests that the photo was taken from the Northeast corner of the Square where City Hall now stands. If correctly identified, this is the only known photograph of the resulting devastation. St. Peter's had been spared.

Photo Courtesy of Jack Lamar Mayfield, *Images of Oxford and Ole Miss*, 2009. From the Patricia Brown Young Collection.

The only remaining photo of original courthouse building (1840), burned by the Union Army in 1864 under the direction of General A.J. "Whiskey" Smith. Union tents are on the grounds before the destruction.

Photo Courtesy of Jack Lamar Mayfield, *Images of Oxford and Ole Miss*, 2009. From the Patricia Brown Young Collection.

3
Post-War Years
1865-1900

The war years had been lean ones for St. Peter's and the University, and their struggles did not end after the war. One of the leaders of the church during the post-war years was Confederate General Francis A. Shoup, a West Point graduate. When the University re-opened its doors in October 1865, Shoup was called to teach mathematics. Of the six new faculty members, three were clergymen. Bishop Green commented at Shoup's ordination to the priesthood in 1868, *"It is hoped that Mr. Shoup will take the parish under his charge and give it as much of attention as he conscientiously can without neglecting his previous, though less important, duties to the University."*

He served as Rector until September 1869, when he resigned and left for Sewanee. Senior Warden Pegues' membership report in 1870 listed 16 families, 41 communicants, 7 Sunday School teachers, and 40 pupils worshipping at St. Peter's.

In the destitution following the Civil War, there was a real danger that the parishioners would lose ownership of the church building because of unpaid bills to builder William Turner. He sued the church for his money. The lawsuit led Frances Devereux Skipwith, daughter of Louisiana Bishop Leonidas Polk and wife of the senior warden, P. H. Skipwith, to seek far and wide for aid in discharging this debt. Response came from Miss Mary Cox of St. Peter's in Germantown, Pennsylvania, but before the money arrived, the debt was settled locally. Miss Cox did not want her gift returned, so the $2,000 she sent to repay the debt was used in 1882 to help build a rectory next door to the church. A receipt located in the church files, dated October 1881, and signed by Senior Warden Pegues, shows the church as having received an additional gift from Mrs. F.D. Skipwith, three United States 4% consols of $500 each and one 4% consol of $100, all to be used "solely for the purpose of erecting a Rectory." These bonds would pay perpetual interest and had no maturity date.

Col. Peyton H. Skipwith, Senior Warden, 1885-1897

Two prominent laymen during the post-bellum period were Colonel Thomas E.B. Pegues and Colonel Peyton H. Skipwith. Col. Pegues, lay delegate at the 1862 General Council, acted as lay reader from 1865 to 1868, and 1869 to 1874, when there were no ministers here. He also served as Senior Warden numerous times. Bishop Green paid this tribute to Pegues on his death: *"The life of this congregation has for some years been preserved by the labors of a faithful and untiring lay reader, Mr. Thomas E.B. Pegues."* Col. Skipwith, lawyer, planter, soldier, pioneer, and one of the founders of the Diocese of Mississippi, served as senior warden from 1885 to 1897. When he died in 1897, Bishop Thompson told the congregation, *"As a loyal churchman and devoted friend of his pastor and his Bishop, he illustrated those traditions equally."*

Two important events in the life of St. Peter's in 1871 were the official consecration of the church and the establishment of St. Peter's Cemetery for "the good people of Oxford," as noted in Jacob Thompson's handwritten deed. Thompson deeded, for the sum of $1, six acres of land to the congregation for the cemetery. A copy of the April 7, 1871, legal document, which gives authority to the Wardens and Vestry of St. Peter's, is on file in the church archives. Visitors to the cemetery today can find the piece of land Thompson retained for family members encircled by a low post-and chain fence under ancient cedar trees.

In her last will and testament, dated 1899, Catherine Thompson left $1000 to St. Peter's for the upkeep of the gravesites of her parents, John N. Peyton Jones and Tabitha Whatley Jones, and her brother, Thomas Jones. Jacob and Catherine Thompson are buried in Memphis, not in St. Peter's Cemetery.

A thorough examination of the complex church/city agreement as to ownership and maintenance of the cemetery is recorded in parishioner Jean Kiger's 2008 work, *A History of St. Peter's Cemetery*, a copy of which is available in the Skipwith Room of the Oxford Lafayette County Library and in St. Peter's archives.

Another Thompson, unrelated to Jacob, appeared in Oxford in the 1880s, and left his mark here and over the diocese. He was The Right Reverend Hugh Miller Thompson, who came to the diocese in 1883 as assistant bishop to Bishop Green, who was then 85 years old. Thompson, born in County Londonderry, Ireland, in 1830, brought with him impressive credentials as a preacher and as a noted author and editor of religious journals. St. Peter's security box contains signed copies of his *Copy: Essays from an Editor's Drawer*, 3rd edition 1885, and *More Copy: Essays from an Editor's Drawer*, 1st edition, 1897, both gifts from Kate Skipwith.

Bishop Hugh Miller Thompson,
2nd Bishop of the Diocese of Mississippi, 1887-1902

Churches all over the South were wrestling with the new status of black people, and the Episcopal Church was no exception. Perhaps responding to Bishop Green's 1883 circular calling for a conference on the relations of the Church to the late slave population, he was committed to work among the Negroes of the state. A man of vision and energy and excellent command of the English language, he gave a stirring address to the diocesan council in 1884 with these words: *"More than half living Mississippians are black people. Is the Church's commission to white people only? We have not a single Negro congregation in the Diocese. Is it wise? Is it Christian?"*

John Crews wrote in his *Goodly Heritage* that the words spoken by the bishop were prophetic when he predicted that a day of reckoning would come if the church neglected its duty to its black neighbors.

As a result of Bishop Thompson's determination to establish a cathedral, St. Peter's was chosen in 1883 to be the first cathedral in the diocese, a position it held until 1889. Thompson moved to Oxford in 1883, and named The Reverend Melville M. Moore, rector of St. Peter's, as Dean of the Cathedral. When Bishop Thompson later moved to the bishop's new home on the Battle Hill property in Jackson, he saw that a new cathedral was built there as a memorial to Bishop Green.

The Rev. Melville Moore, Rector and Dean of the Cathedral 1883-1884
Photo Courtesy of Meg Faulkner Duchaine

When The Rev. Moore moved to Tennessee in 1884, The Rev. Edward Lewis came to St. Peter's and served as Dean of the Cathedral until 1886, when he resigned and moved to Nebraska. The Diocesan Journal of 1885 mentions the parochial report that included a reference to the Children's Guild of St. Peter's and the Guild of St. Andrew. Shortly after The Rev. Lewis left, Mr. John A. Harris was ordained deacon in October 1886, and placed in charge of the Cathedral. On Quinquagesima Sunday (the Sunday before Ash Wednesday) 1887, The Rev. Mr. Harris was advanced to the priesthood by Bishop Thompson. He remained at St. Peter's until 1888, when he went to California for one year. He then returned to St. Peter's in 1889, and stayed for three more years until taking charge of the church in Pass Christian, Mississippi.

St. Peter's was again without a permanent clergyman for several years, leaving The Rev. Herbert Bowers, a missionary, and The Rev. Peter G. Sears, a member of the 1885 graduating class at the University, temporarily in charge. Like his father, who was also an Episcopal Priest, Sears had served as Dean at St. Thomas Hall in Holly Springs. Mr. C. F. McRae filled the position of lay reader from 1892 to 1896. The Rev. E.A. Neville was listed as missionary in the 1899 diocesan report and as rector in 1900.

The parish had no priest until 1903 when The Rev. C.D. Brown arrived. This serious shortage of clergy, however, was not just a problem for the Episcopal Church in Oxford. Poverty and dislocation after the war, and then illness and death from yellow fever near the end of the century, compounded the problem. An article in the August 15, 1878, edition of the New York Times described the "Horrors of Yellow Fever" and how it had severely reduced the population of nearby Grenada, Mississippi. Bishop Thompson also reflected on earlier vacancies, when he spoke to the clergy on his 10th anniversary: *"Some of our most important parishes were vacant. From Oxford to State Line on the Central Road, there was but one clergyman."*

After guiding the diocese for nearly 40 years through war and difficult financial times, Mississippi's first Bishop and the oldest living Bishop in the American Church, The Right Reverend William Mercer Green died in 1887, while serving as Chancellor of the University of the South. His journal entries described his many visits to St. Peter's where he had laid the groundwork for this new church in Oxford, stressing its important connection to the University of Mississippi. St. Columb's Cathedral, championed by Bishop Thompson as a memorial to Bishop Green, was consecrated in 1894. When Bishop Thompson died in 1902, he was buried in St. Columb's Chapel, Battle Hill. When the chapel burned, his body was moved to the cemetery at the Chapel of the Cross in Madison.

While the exact dates of these photos are unknown, it was after 1883 when the spire was added and before the roads were paved in the early 1920s.
Photos provided by Dr. T.J. Ray

4

First Half of a New Century
1900-1956

Upon The Reverend Clement Brown's arrival at St. Peter's in 1903, there were 19 families, 32 communicants, 3 teachers, and 17 pupils listed in St. Peter's Parochial Report. The Rev. Brown served as Rector until 1916, making him the first rector to serve any length of time at St. Peter's. Little information, however, has been found to document activities during his tenure. Parochial reports list numbers and, interestingly, the number of communicants rose steadily from 32 in 1903, to 65 in 1910, then started a decline to only 33 when The Rev. Brown left in 1916. The church had lost two long term wardens and church leaders with the earlier death of P.A. Skipwith in 1897 and C. H. Keys in 1912. Keys had served as Senior Warden from 1898 until his death and was lovingly remembered by his church with the following memorial:

"Mr. Keys was for fourteen years the Senior Warden of St. Peter's Church, Oxford: a man with firm convictions, and the courage to express them....His constant presence at services, and his faithful devotion to the church he loved so much, were of the

personal qualities of his character. He was always active in the things that concerned the public good, and consequently was beloved by all."

The loss of these prominent members of St. Peter's undoubtedly had an impact on this small parish. Also, the United States entered World War I the year after The Rev. Brown left. Interestingly, unlike later references to the impact of World War II, no mention of this first war has been located in church records. We know that the University cancelled commencement in 1917, and granted degrees to those students in good standing when they enlisted. Members of the faculty were given leaves of absence for military service and war work of the Young Men's Christian Association. It is likely that these developments also had an impact on church growth during this time.

The Rev. Sterling Gunn came soon after The Rev. Brown left, but served as rector for only one year, 1918-1919, before his death in 1920. St. Peter's was again without a rector for three years. Another member of the Pegues family, Mr. J. E. Pegues, assumed leadership roles during this time. He served as warden from 1912 until 1925, and was listed in the journals as being lay reader and clerk. Joe Pegues, Jr., followed in his father's footsteps and served as warden from 1931 until 1948.

The Rev. Bradner Moore, ordained to the Deaconate at Sewanee in July 1923, came immediately to St. Peter's, and was ordained to the Priesthood here on December 19 of that same year. Kiger's research uncovered important documentation about this period from St. Peter's 1899 Record Book, held with other original materials in the safe deposit box at First National Bank. The Rev. Moore's entries reveal much about the state of the church when he arrived:

"July 1923. There were no records kept except scattered and spasmodic entrees of Baptisms, Confirmations, Marriages & Burials from the opening of this book until 1923…. Church roof is in need of repair. Exposed woodwork needs paint—gutters and down pipes are nearly destroyed by rust. Furnace is in bad shape and needs new stack. Organ is in need of repairs and adjustment. Brass work in Chancel is terribly tarnished. Brick work needs a lot of repointing and the buttresses require replastering. Pews need replacing. Carpet is badly worn." He added, however, *"With all its lack, St. Peter's is a beautiful monument to the Glory of God and the memory of those who dreamed it, and materialized the dream." Bradner J. Moore, Deacon.*

In October 1923, the parish decided to petition Bishop Coadjutor Green to put St. Peter's on mission status. This was officially accomplished in November and St. Peter's remained dependent on the Diocese for the next thirty-nine years.

The Rev. Moore was instrumental in attracting Methodists Arthur Palmer Hudson and John Falkner into the congregation. Parish records reveal that John and Lucille (Dolly) Falkner, formerly Methodists, were confirmed at St. Peter's on December 14, 1924. Notes from an undated interview with the rector contain Dolly Falkner's description of Moore as a "big, brawny man, a true minister; if you were not at church on Sunday, he was out to see you on Monday." She described his wife as being from a "prominent Bairdstown, Mississippi family and educated in Europe, but dressed out of the missionary box." The missionary box was a program of the National Church that collected and distributed clothes to those working in the mission field.

Crews wrote that Hudson, a noted folklorist from the University of North Carolina, served as a lay preacher at St. Peter's and delivered a Christmas sermon sometime between 1923 and 1929, a portion of which follows:

"Our presence here this morning in this quiet and gracious old church is one of the best proofs in all the world that the spirit of Christ lives. For what civilization but a Christian civilization would have brought us here – the children of simple farmers, shopkeepers, country doctors, county-seat lawyers, teachers, artisans, and parents in all the other simple callings of our national life – what civilization but a Christian civilization would have exempted us in these years of physical vigor from the hard toil of our fathers and mothers, to give us a chance equal to that enjoyed by the wealthiest and most fortunate – a chance to make our lives rich and significant? What civilization would sprinkle a great country with hospitals and other foundations for the relief of the sick and unfortunate? The better we understand Him, the more, not the less, miraculous seems Jesus...His was the first mind of all the ages to think in terms of universal humanity – to think of all mankind as one family, a vast but nonetheless intimate and mutually responsible brotherhood of God as loving Father; of the Kingdom of Heaven as within the hearts of men; of saving one's life by giving it away to others."

An industrious man, The Rev. Moore's contributions in the diocese are well documented in *The Episcopal Church in Mississippi: 1763-1992.*

He directed the first church camp for young people in 1924, at the Gulf Coast Military Academy, located between Biloxi and Gulfport. His assistant was a young University of Mississippi student, Girault Jones, also a lay reader at St. Peter's, who would later become Bishop of Louisiana. In 1926, Moore directed the second camp near Durant called Camp Bratton. Bishop T. D. Bratton and Bishop William Mercer Green II were often present, thus the official name became Camp Bratton Green, as it is still called today. St. Peter's parish family continues to provide strong leadership for the popular camp. Before The Rev. Moore left St. Peter's in 1927, the communicant list had doubled. Almost twenty years after he left St. Peter's, he was appointed the 1st Diocesan Chairman of the Army and Navy Commission, an organization responsible for ministry to service personnel across the country during World War II.

Following Bradner Moore as rector was Dr. Edward McCrady (1928-1939), described by Crews as having brought a degree of erudition to the preaching. McCrady came to Oxford just as the Great Depression was settling over the town, and political forces led by Gov. Theodore Bilbo were trying to consolidate and move the University.

Dr. McCrady was chairman of the philosophy department on campus. He preached long sermons, according to parishioner Nevin Jones, and this presented a problem for students who wanted to get to Gordon Hall, the University boarding house, in time to be served Sunday dinner. The Jones story has been told many times. You had to be there by 1:30 or there was no food left. So Nevin and his brother Pipes decided to ask Dr. McCrady if he could shorten his sermons a little so they could make it to Sunday dinner in time. Dr. McCrady told the brothers Jones, *"I will cut the music; I will cut the prayers; but I will not cut my sermons."*

Dr. and Mrs. McCrady's son John, who achieved recognition as a regionalist painter, spent his formative years in Oxford, soaking up sights and experiences he was later to put down on canvas. Their daughter Isabel later became the wife of the fifth Bishop of Mississippi, The Rt. Rev. Duncan M. Gray, the mother of the 7th Bishop, The Rt. Rev. Duncan M. Gray, Jr., and the grandmother of the 9th Bishop, The Rt. Rev. Duncan M. Gray III.

Dr. McCrady also figures in the subject of William Faulkner's association with St. Peter's. Dr. McCrady refused to marry Estelle Oldham Franklin and William Faulkner because of the church's stand against divorce at the time. McCrady told the couple if they came back after a year's probation, they would be welcome at services. They were married at College Hill Presbyterian Church (on the porch, according to local lore, for the same reasons concerning divorce) on June 20, 1929. After a year's probation, the couple began attending St. Peter's – William not as often as Estelle. Bob Farley, former Dean of the University of Mississippi Law School, told John Crews in 1975 that Faulkner considered himself a member of St. Peter's. Bishop Gray, Jr, rector in the 60s, said the same, and that Faulkner sometimes read the lesson at church and pledged to St. Peter's. Excerpts from Bishop Gray's address at the Faulkner Centennial in 1997 are included in this manuscript's later section, Facts and Legends.

The church's close relationship with the University was strengthened even more by The Rev. McCrady's presence. McCrady had come to St. Peter's just three years after the famous Scopes trial in Dayton, Tennessee had brought national attention to the teaching of the theory of evolution. Dr. William Morse, Professor of Geology at the university, remarked upon McCrady's death, "...his ministry was the ministry of a leader—the leader the University student so badly needs and so seriously craves. His greatest service was to lead the students to the heights of understanding that there is no conflict between science and religion—that true science like true religion leads to God."

In 1939, The Rev. William Mercer Green, Jr., great-grandson of the 1st Bishop of Mississippi and son of the then-current Bishop Green, came to St. Peter's and served as rector until 1943, when he was called to WWII as an Air Force Chaplain. He returned from the war in 1945. In his January 1946 address to Annual Council, Bishop Duncan Gray welcomed The Rev. Green home with these words, *"We welcome Chaplain Green back home and rejoice with the congregation and University students that we will now have through his good offices a full time ministry in this important center."*

The Bishop then thanked The Rev. Charles Liles and the vestry at All Saints in Grenada for taking care of the vacant parish in Oxford. Green was called back to service in October 1948.

Before The Rev. Green returned to service, he attended the 120th

Diocesan Council in January 1947. Former rector Bradner Moore, now retired but chairing the College Works Commission, talked of changes in college ministry. Moore's report is important to St. Peter's history because of the close connection between the church and the University and the importance the Diocese placed on the church's presence on campus. Moore said, *"The work in this field has undergone two notable changes in 1946. The Rev. William Mercer Green has returned to the leading student project of the Diocese, at the University. During Mr. Green's leaves for service... his charge was vacant. The increase in student registration that has followed the return of many service men to civil life, has added to the urgent necessity of the church's ministry at Oxford...."*

Moore also spoke of a campus ministry for Negroes. It had been more than 60 years since The Rev. Hugh Miller Thompson addressed the Diocesan Council with his thoughts on our responsibility to the former slave population. Moore continued, *"A rounded out college program ought to include a campus ministry for Negroes. Of course one is being realized at Okolona Industrial School. Alcorn A & M offers an invitation to a racial college ministry. It would seem desirable to assign the Negro college field, as a whole, to a specially prepared pastor, who would include in his care such colleges as those at Jackson, Tougaloo, Utica, and Edwards."* Still, it would be another fifteen years before the Chaplain at the University of Mississippi would have the opportunity to minister to a Negro student after the enrollment of James Meredith.

Moore described the challenges of ministering to students after WWII. *"Conditions on the campus, in these days of feverish living, have changed the possibilities of ministering to the spiritual needs of students. Except for a very few students and faculty members, the old forums and clubs of another day have no appeal. It remains to do personal counseling, and to attract student congregations on Sunday morning with challenging sermons. This means, as a prime requirement, that the college pastor must put serious thought into the preparation of his message. His inner conviction and sincerity will earn for him the confidence of his college congregations."*

Thus, Moore, the first camp director while rector at St. Peter's, was still making his mark on the student population being watched over by the Diocese and the small church in Oxford.

Postcard from McCrady Scrapbook,
Church Archives & UM Special Collections

With The Rev. Green back in military service, The Rev. William Asger came in May 1949, in time to be heavily involved in St. Peter's preparations for its 1951 Centennial Celebration. To commemorate this historic occasion, The Rev. Asger compiled the first church history, *A History of St. Peter's Episcopal Church 1851-1951.* The strong ties between the University and St. Peter's were again emphasized in a letter to Asger and the Vestry from Chancellor J.D. Williams:

"For a hundred years St. Peter's Church in Oxford and the University of Mississippi have been good and friendly neighbors, sharing the same hardships, enjoying the same satisfactions which come from worthwhile service, and at times led by mutual personnel. Dr. Frederick A.P. Barnard, President of the University from 1856 to 1859 and chancellor from then until 1861, was ordained an Episcopal priest in Oxford on December 2, 1855, and became the first Rector of St. Peter's. It is reported that slaves owned by Jacob Thompson, a member of the Board of Trustees from 1844-1857 and its president from 1852-1856, made the brick and built the church....We extend warmest and good wishes for its continued high quality of service to the community, its spiritual leadership, and its lofty tradition."

In his 1951 journal entry, Bishop Gray, Sr. recorded the events of the Centennial Celebration: *"April 7: By train to Batesville where The Rev. Asger met me and drove me to Oxford. During the afternoon looked over the remodeled rectory which now contains parish house and upstairs apartment. Reception held at night and parish house dedicated. On April 8: ...confirmed 30 and preached. Purse offering $67.80...Home on the City of New Orleans following a wonderful weekend."* According to the April 1951 church newsletter, 25 of the 30 confirmed were University faculty or students.

The need for a rectory was crucial. The Committee on Bishops, hoping that the women of the Diocese would undertake this project, offered this resolution at the 1952 Annual Council:

"BE IT RESOLVED, that this Council commend the Women's auxiliary of the Diocese and the Laymen's League for their untiring work and encouraging support in the program of the Church and further commend to them the need of a rectory at St. Peter's church, Oxford as a possible project for the coming year."

The first Bishop Duncan Gray, in his address at Council, spoke not only of the need of a rectory in Oxford, but the Diocesan responsibility in supporting this undertaking: *"To me the most pressing need and not to be put off need in the Diocese is a rectory for St. Peter's Church, Oxford. The old rectory, with so many hallowed associations, has been converted into an adequate parish house and student center which means that we must acquire a rectory. I have conferred with the rector and vestry at Oxford and they are anxious to build a suitable rectory and the congregation will give substantially and liberally to the cause. Our work at Ole Miss, however, is recognized as a responsibility of the National Church and Diocese, and I am going to call upon the Diocese – every congregation in the Diocese – to make gifts to the Oxford Rectory Fund. Without any effort to speak of, you gave nine or ten thousand dollars to the Student Center at Starkville and I am sure you will want to have a large part in improving our facilities and increasing the effectiveness of our work at the University of Mississippi. Last year The Rev. William Asger presented 30 candidates for confirmation most of whom were faculty members and students. The local congregation, which is really generous beyond its means, will set us all a real example in giving and interest."*

The Rev. William Asger, Rector 1949-1953

The number of communicants in 1952 was reported at 142, twenty-three of whom were confirmed during the Bishop's visit on April 27 of that year. The church was definitely growing in numbers. The Rev. Asger was known for his brief sermons, unlike McCrady's that reportedly caused the Jones brothers to miss many Sunday meals.

Before The Rev. Emile Joffrion came in 1954, the vestry had decided to buy a rectory instead of building one. The Diocese helped by paying $3,000 on a $10,000 loan along with the interest. Bishop Gray did not ask the diocese to launch an official campaign to cover the balance of $7,000, but he did, in his 1953 Diocesan address, ask that members devise ways and means to take care of this debt during the year. He said, *"Certainly we should be able to distribute it in such a way as to give everybody a chance to have a part in our ministry at Ole Miss where we probably have more Episcopalians enrolled than in all the other Mississippi colleges combined."*

After settling his young family in the new rectory, The Rev. Joffrion turned to overseeing the building of a new parish house. The 1956 campaign had a goal of $75,000. Details on this project are included in Chapter 8, "The Land and the Building." Joffrion may have been the first rector at St. Peter's to speak out on a local racial issue. The University refused to allow the Reverend Alvin Kershaw, a pro-NAACP Episcopal priest to speak on campus. University history professor Charles Eagles describes Joffrion's stand: *"In Oxford, A. Emile Joffrion, the priest at St. Peter's, regretted that some Mississippians wanted to refuse to let the University be the University. The 'infantile and petty measures' used by Kershaw's opponents to keep him from the campus would, according to Joffrion, cause irreparable damages."*

Joffrion then openly supported sociology professor Morton King who resigned in protest of Kerhshaw's cancelled invitation.

The Emile Joffrion Family 1954-1957

Glimpse of the Parish from Parochial Reports to the Diocese of Mississippi:

1954: Members in good standing=138 Pledges=$6,119
1955: Members in good standing=155 Pledges=$7,231
1956: Members in good standing=145 Pledges=$7,325

Bishop Duncan M. Gray, Jr., 7th Bishop of the Diocese of Mississippi, 1974-
1993. Rector at St. Peter's: 1957-1965

5

The Turbulent 60s and 70s

The Reverend Duncan M. Gray, Jr. came to Oxford in 1957 from Cleveland, Mississippi, his first assignment after his 1953 graduation from seminary. Having been on mission status since 1923, St. Peter's enjoyed a steady growth of membership under Gray's leadership, and he was instrumental in the mission church becoming a parish again in January 1962. The church reported members in good standing at 145 in 1956, and by the end of 1961, when the formal application to become St. Peter's Episcopal Church was sent to Bishop Duncan Gray from The Rev. Duncan Gray, Jr., there were 220 members in good standing. The budget had also increased from $7,325 in 1956, to a modified one of $23,000 in 1961. The mission church was no longer dependent upon the Diocese. When Diocesan approval came on November 3, 1961, to become a Parish, an important organizational meeting was held in the "Parish House Student Center" on December 5, 1961. The Parish Constitution approved at that meeting is on file in the church office. A list of confirmed male persons over 21 years of age was sent to members for vestry consideration. Women were not allowed to serve on the vestry at that time.

In addition to serving as Rector, Bishop Gray was Chaplain to the Ole Miss Students and advisor to their Canterbury Fellowship Club until The Rev. Wofford Smith came as the first assistant rector/chaplain in 1961. Gray continued the traditions of Bishops Otey and Green, quoted earlier in this text as *"to give immediate attention to"* and *"to take care of ...sons of the Church...to preserve them from the temptations of college life...."* These concerns continued, now for both sons and daughters of families across the state, as reported by Mrs. Gloria Bottom, president of the Episcopal Church Women, Diocese of Mississippi. She wrote, *"College work is on the move in Mississippi. The year 1961 marked the establishment of the first full time College Chaplaincy in our Diocese, as The Rev. Wofford K. Smith began his work on the University of Mississippi campus."*

The Rev. Smith, perhaps realizing the influence of the women's organization, wrote: *"Whether or not we succeed in this field will depend upon our Churchwomen. They have always been a real spark in providing impetus for any major effort we have ever undertaken."* Smith left in 1964, and eventually assumed a leadership role in the nation's college chaplaincy program before he retired as Chaplain Emeritus at the University of Maryland in 1986. He died in 1990.

In a 2009 interview by Dr. Charles Reagan Wilson, Director of the Center for the Study of Southern Culture at The University of Mississippi, the now retired second Bishop Duncan Gray shared memories of his time at St. Peter's. He spoke of the important role the two ministerial associations, one black, one white, played when they joined forces and opened an important channel of communication to both black and white citizens of Oxford during the difficult time leading up to James Meredith's admission to the University. Gray described the joint ministerial group as being the voice of reason for bringing peace and order to Oxford and for providing a critical means of communication between the black and white communities. He commented on St. Peter's current relationship with Second Baptist Church, started while his son, present Bishop Duncan M. Gray, III, was rector at St. Peter's (1985-2000). Shared activities such as pulpit swaps, hymn singings, and tailgate picnics in the Grove before football games continue today.

James Meredith's enrollment at The University of Mississippi in

1962 had a profound effect on The Reverend Gray and St. Peter's as reflected in his sermons leading up to and after the tragic riot the evening of September 30, 1962. On that fateful Sunday morning, the rector spoke these words from the pulpit at St. Peter's: *"The atmosphere of a Church is one of peace and quiet… and this has been hard to find in Oxford during the past two weeks. It might be well, then, for us to take advantage of this hour to give some calm and prayerful thought to our present situation. Could we, then, for a few moments this morning, consider reverently and rationally just where we are, where we are headed, and what we as Christians are doing about it? I think we should ask ourselves, first of all, if we are really sufficiently aware of the **deadly serious** nature of our present predicament."*

Later that evening, the riots broke out, leaving two people dead and untold damage to The University of Mississippi. Gray continued his sermon on that fateful morning with these words: *"And I do not believe that any one of us here today could stand in the presence of Jesus of Nazareth, look him squarely in the eye, and say we will not admit a Negro to the University of Mississippi."* He closed this difficult sermon with a plea to the congregation that everyone *"ask for God's guidance and direction that we may faithfully fulfill our responsibility to the end that God's will may be done."*

One week later, on Sunday, October 7, Gray addressed the parishioners with these opening words: *"As most of you know, the clergy of the Oxford-University community have called upon churches throughout the state to make this Sunday a special occasion for repentance and turning from the tragic events of last Sunday night and Monday morning. For most of us here today those events seem like a terrible nightmare that we would never have believed possible…. I'm sure that all of us here today feel depressed, burdened, and sorrowful; as, indeed, we should. But, as Christians, we cannot let our reaction stop at this point. Fundamental to the Christian faith is the profound conviction that even out of the worst tragedy, some good can come; that light can be born out of darkness; that there can be an Easter for every Good Friday."*

In 1962, the church budget suffered along with decreased attendance. In April, the canvass committee had reported that 116 pledges totaling $25,888 had been made, but in the year's end report on December 17, 1962, the treasurer warned of impending budget problems unless pledge payments caught up with pledged amounts.

Bishop Gray shared an interesting account of how old friends came to St. Peter's rescue during the annual Every Member Canvas: *"Oscar Carr,* a friend from Clarksdale who also was in charge of Diocesan Stewardship, called to ask how he might help. He offered to come to St. Peter's annual pledge campaign dinner and speak. 'What if I bring Farley Salmon with me?'" he asked Gray.

Farley had been a most popular Ole Miss quarterback, and was still an important and respected voice in Mississippi. Salmon and Carr came and spoke, not about race, but to show support for Gray and St. Peter's. This was interesting, Gray noted, since half of the coaching staff at Ole Miss had been members of St. Peter's and many had pulled out over the integration issue. Gray mentioned two by name who stayed and offered support: Junie Hovious and Doc Knight. The program for the campaign dinner, dated February 1963, contains a letter from Duncan Gray, Jr., with these words of hope: *"These are trying times for our community and our parish; and no one is more aware of this than I. The need for love, compassion, and understanding for our fellow man is, perhaps, greater today than ever before in our time. It is a difficult challenge that we face, but by God's grace, we will be able to meet it."*

The third parishioner Gray mentioned in his interview with Wilson was Dr. Robert Holley, a beloved physician in Oxford, who "tripled his pledge" which amounted to one third of the church budget during this difficult time. Gray spoke fondly of Dr. Holley and his wife, Jeanne, for their dedication to St. Peter's and to the Gray family. Dr. Charles Wilson's complete interview with Bishop Gray, Jr., produced and directed by the University of Mississippi Media and Documentary Projects, is available online.

In November 1962, the same month the vestry elected four new members to replace those who had resigned, The Right Reverend Duncan Gray, Sr., Bishop of Mississippi, and his son, The Rev. Duncan Gray, Jr., received the following telegram from the National Church Council:

"In the light of recent events in Mississippi, the National Council of the Protestant Episcopal Church gratefully takes note that law and order are being restored in that troubled situation. We quote what one of our Mississippi clergy has said, 'None of us can stand in the presence of Jesus of Nazareth, look him squarely in the eye, and say that a Negro should not be admitted to the University of Mississippi.' (Gray's September 30, 1962 sermon.) We affirm our complete agreement with this sense of the uncompromising claim of Christ, and our support of our church people in their obedience to it."

In his conversation with Professor Wilson, Gray recalled approximately one-third of the congregation leaving in protest of his support of the integration of Ole Miss. This group organized a Reformed Anglican Church which met in various locations for three or four years. A more detailed account of Gray's turbulent role in the 1962 crisis may be found in Will Campbell's *And Also With You* (1997) and Araminta Stone Johnston's *And One Was a Priest* (2011).

Dr. Robert Holley addressed the parish at the 1963 annual meeting with these words: *"It is the opinion of the vestry that The Reverend Duncan Gray, Jr. has conducted the affairs of this parish with intelligence and dedication, faithfully and prayerfully. Many changes are occurring in America …changes which we, as members of the Body of Christ…have seen and known were coming. With the help of God and with mutual love, counsel and the guidance of a dedicated ministry, we will be able to meet the changes and live in the future in such a manner as to reflect Christian charity and honor on this parish, this community, and this nation."*

Dr. Holley had served as Senior Warden during this turbulent time (1960-1964), and in 1985, seven years after his death, his wife, Jeanne Holley, became the first woman Senior Warden at St. Peter's.

The women of St. Peter's continued to be active and supportive during these difficult times. Their directories from the decade of the 60s described "The Women of St. Peter's" as an overall organization for all women in the church. Many chose to be more active by taking part in monthly guild meetings: St. Anne's met in the morning, St. Catherine's met in the afternoon, and the Kate Skipwith Guild met in the evening. These annual directories outlined the group's mission and included an annual calendar and noted churchwomen with guild membership. The historical listing in the 1963 year book of the Episcopal Churchwomen Diocese of Mississippi identified Mrs. Hugh Miller Thompson as the organization's first president in 1891. There were 108 women communicants at St. Peter's in 1963. They were charged with visiting new or prospective members, visiting the ill, and notifying the rector of any good or bad news concerning a member or friend of St. Peter's. For many years, the women, working with other churches in an Inter-Church Council, operated a clothes closet for needy families.

In March 1964, an overall Parish Survey Committee made a report to the vestry of the results of their evaluation of parish unity in which the purpose of the church was defined. A major part of the survey dealt with the division of church services which would allow university students access to the University Chaplain and the members of St. Peter's the "constant ministry of their rector." The Chaplain held one service a month in St. Peter's during this period. When Wofford Smith left in 1964, the position was vacant until William Morris came in 1966 as the second Chaplain to serve in this capacity. The chaplain's office was now located on the 3rd floor of the "Y" Building, one of the remaining antebellum buildings on campus.

In 1965, the Rev. and Mrs. Gray and their four children moved to Meridian where he became rector of St. Paul's. Following Gray, Jr. in the pulpit at St. Peter's was The Rev. Hugh McDonald "Don" Morse, Jr., who served as rector from 1965 until 1974. His attempts to engage the parish are evident from various reports and vestry minutes. In October 1966, each new member of the parish was escorted by a vestry member to a High Tea. Each vestry member was responsible to get other parishioners to attend. He proposed monthly suppers, the beginnings of the popular Supper Club which continued almost 40 years until it outgrew itself and homes could no longer accommodate the number of parishioners participating.

More than 20 years before Leap Frog was officially launched in 1989, the vestry passed a motion in October 1967 to offer a tutoring program for public school students two afternoons a week. Attempts to document the success or longevity of this early program have been unsuccessful.

Miss Kate Skipwith, a long-time supporter of St. Peter's, had died in 1961, and left the church a handsome bequest of more than $100,000. The first $50,000 of this gift had been received in March 1963. Using some of the funds from the final payment from the Skipwith bequest ($54,620 less 10% attorney fees), St. Peter's purchased the Price Street house in 1966 as a home for the new Assistant Rector/Chaplain, William Morris. This was the year Canterbury Club members were busy analyzing the Beatles "Yellow Submarine" in an attempt to increase participation in their activities. They were also making plans to open a coffeehouse above Sneed's Hardware on the Square.

In April 1966, the Committee for Evaluation of the Worship Program presented their recommendations, the first being to keep Morning

Prayer as the basic service and not to celebrate Holy Communion so frequently as to render it commonplace. The committee also addressed getting the "whole hearted involvement of the participants: responses made with vigor and hymns given full voice (perhaps the old familiar hymns should not be neglected), and securing a maximum atmosphere of worship with music coordinated with the order of service."

Financial problems continued to plague the church throughout the late 60s and the vestry had been forced to absorb the cemetery funds into the general fund earlier in 1967, so that the three-month assessment and quota to the Diocese could be made. This assessment continued to be a financial burden for another year while the vestry discussed the advantages of reverting to mission status. The Rev. Morse took the position that changing back to a mission would not solve the problems unless a reduction in assessment was negotiated. In 1967, eight families were covering 33% of the budget, and seventeen families covered 50%.

In 1968, The Rev. Morse encouraged parishioners to conduct small group discussions where they might openly express their opinions and concerns. To improve internal communications, he also suggested the creation of a monthly newsletter. The area's first Head Start program began this same year in the parish hall. The Head Start ministry grew out of the Committee on Problems of the Poor, and while some members resisted this program, senior warden Ham Williston posed this question in his 1969 address to the parish, "If Christ were on earth today, what position would He take?" When the Head Start program moved to the Gordon School in Abbeville in August 1970, it contributed to St. Peter's two new air conditioning and heating units for the Student Center and red velvet curtains for the stage. Thirty-four pre-schoolers had benefitted from this program.

Eastview Homes, a multi-million dollar low-rent housing project, was conceived by members of St. Peter's in 1968, in response to national and local unrest following the assassination of Dr. Martin Luther King in Memphis. Church member Loren Young was an indefatigable worker in the establishment of that project. St. Peter's was the sponsoring agent for the program and two members of the governing board were appointed by the vestry for years. The U.S. Department of Housing and Urban Development (HUD) funded the multi-million dollar project, an early example of cooperation between government and a faith-based enterprise. Open House was held in January 1971. The vestry entertained Needs of the Elderly the next month and conducted a senior housing analysis; however, no housing materialized from these early efforts.

In April 1969 the Vestry shared with the parish the following resolution they had voted to send to the Agenda Committee of the 1970 National Convention in Houston: *"...the Protestant Episcopal Church should adopt a policy of never extending support, financial or political, to any individual, group, or organization which seeks to promote Fascism, neo-Nazism, Marxism, Maoism, or any other totalitarian ideology. .. black separatism or supremacy or white separatism or supremacy...."*

This resolution was published again in the October 1970 *Epistle*, an earlier form of the church newsletter. No further explanation was given by the vestry for submitting this resolution, but news releases from the Episcopal News Service from May 1969, report that Council had rejected the Manifesto of the Black Economic Development Conference, and had voted to end involvement with banks participating in the Consortium Credit to South Africa. Council was also planning a World Conference on Religion and Peace in 1970, with ten major world religions. It appears that the vestry at St. Peter's was taking a stand on these critical issues being considered by the Agenda Committee.

The Episcopal presence on campus grew more prominent during the Vietnam era. In his 1969 annual report to St. Peter's, the new Assistant Rector, David Elliot, cited the general attitude of many students who found no meaning in "organized religion." He detailed his efforts to reach them through different forms of experimental worship. Peace services were held in the Grove with campus security always present, "their choice," according to Elliott, who served as Assistant Rector/Chaplain from 1969-1971. An article in the November 13, 1969, *Commercial Appeal*, "War Protests Are Planned on 4 Mississippi Campuses," was uncovered in the electronic archives of the Mississippi Sovereignty Commission. In addition to Ole Miss, other schools mentioned in the article were Mississippi State, Mississippi State College for Women, and Mary Holmes College at West Point.

An experimental folk mass was held on the back porch of the "Y Building," one of the few remaining antebellum buildings on campus and home of religious life. As did the Canterbury Club in 1966, The Rev. Elliott held services using music of Simon and Garfunkel, Bob Dylan, James Taylor, and John Prine in an attempt to connect to the student body. He led a memorial service on May 5, 1970, for the four students killed at Kent State and a second memorial service on May 11 for Warren Edwards, who was killed on his return to campus from a peace rally in Washington. A few members withdrew their pledges to St. Peter's because of these services.

The Rev. Morse was named Diocesan Contact for the Diocese of Mississippi on matters concerning conscientious objection and draft counseling. In a letter to The Rev. Morse dated July 9, 1970, the Executive Council of the Episcopal Church suggested that he contact the Bishop for the Armed Forces to inquire about available materials. Also working on ways to vitalize parish life, The Rev. Morse initiated and the vestry approved in 1972, the formation of five Vestry Task Forces: Christian Education, Finance, Christian Outreach, Sanctuary, and the Physical Plant. The Rev. Morse then helped other parishes in their efforts to implement this organizational structure.

In 1971, the Churchwomen's activities continued and now included operation of the Jewel Box, a "store" set up on Sunday morning to sell goods that they had purchased from the Episcopal Bookshop in Memphis for a slight profit. The goal was to raise enough money to support a child through the Christian Children's Fund. A year later with $42, the church started its support of 11- year old Maria Stella of Brazil. The February 1972 newsletter shared this letter from Maria with the parish:

"Dear Sponsors, I was so happy to receive the $15 you so kindly sent me. With this money I bought a pair of school shoes, a pair of stockings and a beautiful blouse, thank you so very much for remembering me on my birthday and at Christmas time."

The church added more important community activity in 1972, opening a Handicapped Training Center which operated five days a week, with eighteen children enrolled the first year. Fifty University students served as volunteers. Children with cognitive and physical disabilities attended classes in the parish hall from 1972-77. Originally known as Lafayette County Development Center, its name was changed to Oxford Child Development Center when the Oxford School District took it over in 1976. The program continued to be housed at St. Peter's until the fall of

1977, when it moved to the North Mississippi Regional Center. Today it is called the Scott Center, a part of Oxford's Public School District located next to Oxford Middle School, and it serves students from multiple school districts.

The Rev. Morse and his family moved to Pass Christian in 1974. The Rev. A. C. "Chip" Marble, who had replaced The Rev. Elliott in 1971 as Assistant/ Chaplain, was named rector, and Jim McGhee came the next year to replace Marble as Assistant/Chaplain. The next several years were exciting ones for St. Peter's. The church was designated a National Historic Site in 1975, and then celebrated its 125th anniversary in 1976. Celebration activities began with the dedication of a new stained glass window. A baptismal service was held on April 5 in the Lafayette County Courthouse to commemorate the organization of the parish and Oxford's first Episcopal baptisms in 1851. On April 7, a covered dish dinner was followed by a presentation by the Sewanee Choir. *Intruder in the Dust*, with opening scenes in the church, was then shown as the annual Oxford Pilgrimage began. Dr. John Crews, Professor of English at the University, offered his history of St. Peter's, *A Goodly Heritage*, during this anniversary year. Also during this historic year, St. Peter's made a commitment to needs outside the parish through reinvestment of the Skipwith Fund and by assuming leadership roles in community programs such as the Juvenile Shelter, Meals on Wheels, and the Clothes Closet. In his annual report to the parish on December 5, 1976, The Rev. Marble commented on the use of the proposed revised Book of Common Prayer that year. Noting that it had not been an easy transition, the reception of the new rites had been heartening. Annual Council was held at St. Peter's in 1977, a huge event made successful with the help of strong parish leadership.

The Rev. Marble accepted an invitation from Church of the Mediator, Meridian and was installed as their new rector in April 1978. Just as had The Rev. Duncan Gray, Jr. who also went to Meridian from Oxford, Marble later became Bishop of the Diocese of Mississippi – Gray in 1974 and Marble in 1993.

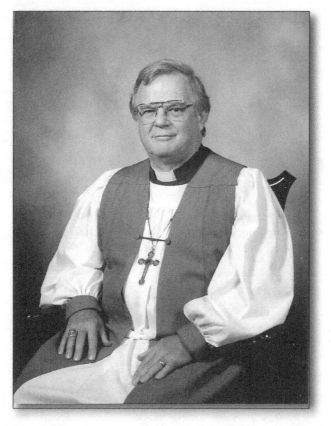

Bishop Alfred Clark Marble Jr., 8th Bishop of the Diocese of Mississippi, 1993-2003. Rector at St. Peter's: 1974-1978

The Revs Wofford Smith, 1st full time chaplain and Chip Marble, rector, The Right Rev. Duncan Gray, Jr, Bishop of Mississippi, The Revs. Fred Bush, Jim McGhee, and Sam Tomlinson at the 125th Celebration.

St. Peter's was designated a national historic site in 1975.
In 1976, the State of Mississippi erected a historical marker to denote the church's historical significance.

6

Another Century Winds Down: 1978-2000

The Rev. Douglas Stirling came to St. Peter's in 1978. In his first meeting with the vestry that August, he announced, "The climate is good here, sense an air of hospitality, a lot of willingness to work." He was joined by The Rev. John-Michael van Dyck, who came the next year as Assistant/Chaplain. The campus ministry's annual report reminded parishioners that while "the Diocese does financially underwrite the program, the ties between St. Peter's and Ole Miss are so close that this is also our parochial mission." This commitment to the University again reinforced that of the first Bishop Green when he spoke of the need of a church near the University and the importance of diocesan-wide support. In a letter dated August 25, 1978, Canon Fred Bush explained the new method of funding the diocesan budget: each parish should report in September the percentage of parochial income it planned to give and then in December report a specific dollar amount.

St. Peter's continued during Stirling's tenure to serve Nativity, the mission church in Water Valley, the jail ministry, Eastview Homes, and Haven House, a local alcohol rehabilitation center. The church sponsored a refugee family from Vietnam in 1979 and a Cambodian family in 1982. In 1981, however, church leaders were again wrestling with financial woes. They decided to use interest from the Skipwith funds to retire church debt and to take a loan the next year to cover operating expenses. Difficult financial times did not prevent the Visitation Committee, made up of thirteen church women, from making a record number of contacts, 1454, and 162 personal calls in 1981.

The Rev. van Dyck left in 1982 and the chaplain position was vacant until The Rev. Paul Stricklin came in March 1984. The average annual pledge that year was $680 and 107 pledges were on record. The church women produced the "Cooky Book" and sold it for $1 a copy, with proceeds earmarked for Christian Education.

A profile of St. Peter's compiled in August 1984 provided the following membership breakdown: 196 households, 409 baptized members and 372 communicants. The largest single group was retirees (45). The number of UM faculty (43) and staff (30) reflected the strong connection to the University that Bishops Otey and Green had encouraged in the beginning. The profile did not include numbers for University students. An interesting comparison may be made to the report in 1924, which showed 17 families, 28 communicants, and 40 university students.

Since The Rev. Stirling had recently moved to Mobile, The Rev. Paul Stricklin served both St. Peter's and the Episcopal Students at Ole Miss from March 1984 until the new rector arrived on February 1, 1985. The Rev. Duncan M. Gray III, a teenager when his father, Duncan Gray, Jr., moved the family from Oxford to Meridian's St. Paul's in 1965, would now be leading parishioners, some of whom had watched him grow up in the church. Having planned to be a teacher or a coach, the younger Gray came home to lead St. Peter's through a time of unprecedented growth, until he, too, would leave to become Bishop of the Episcopal Diocese of Mississippi. In a February 28, 2000, interview he remarked that his dad had been one of his role models, but that they were different; they approached things differently. "His style wouldn't necessarily be my style, but his influence has been significant," he told *The Oxford Eagle* reporter.

Still receiving support from the Diocese and with an office in the historic "Y" Building on campus, the presence of the Episcopal Church at Ole Miss remained strong. The Rev. Hal Hutchinson came as Chaplain in 1987, followed by The Rev. Kee Sloan in 1990. With help from a Diocesan grant, St. Peter's established Leap Frog, an after-school tutorial program for at-risk elementary students in 1989. The program was headquartered at St. Peter's and parishioner Kris Mink served as its first director. Generous parishioners provided scholarships to insure that the first thirteen children from Bramlett Elementary School's first and second grades would receive much needed tutoring. That program now enjoys strong tutorial support from University students, members of the church, and many townspeople. By 2011, the program was jointly sponsored by St. Peter's, Oxford-University United Methodist, and United Way, and students were receiving tutoring at both sponsoring churches and Lafayette Elementary School. Looking back to 1967, the vestry had voted to allow a tutoring program for public school students, two days a week, 3:30 to 5:00. In 1970, The Rev. Elliott had received approval to allow two University students use of two or three rooms for tutoring 18 black students, grades 1-6. It had taken many years to sufficiently fund and support a permanent tutoring program.

In 1989, Habitat for Humanity completed its first house in the community and St. Peter's was largely responsible for its success. The Rev. Duncan Gray III provided hands-on leadership for this new community outreach program, as did several members of the parish. Support to the Pantry was ongoing, as was the Jail Ministry which supplied a library for the inmates. The 11th Honduras Mission trip in 1993, coordinated by St. Peter's, saw 3,157 patients at the medical clinic, 526 at the dental clinic, and wrote 9,224 prescriptions. In addition, the veterinarians treated 687 horses and 50 dogs! Members of St. Peter's continue to be in the forefront of this mission, and will assume sponsorship of the mission again in 2011-2012.

Programs such as "St. Peter's Friends of Music," Older Adults Ministry, Jr. Choir, Jr. EYC, Tuesday morning Bible Study, and the first Mardi Gras Parade and Retiring of the Alleluia Banner in 1990, provided opportunities for students and local resident members alike to become involved in an active parish life.

In October 1994, the church named a building committee to oversee construction of a new addition and renovation of existing spaces. In 1993, the Parish Redevelopment Task Force had recommended repairs on the existing building, kitchen renovation, and more educational space as its top three priorities. This $417,000 project began on April 3, 1995. The new wing was dedicated a year later on March 31. A columbarium was also constructed in 1996. More details on these projects are included in Chapter 8, "The Land and the Building." Happily, pledges exceeded the budget that busy year. Also in 1996, St. Peter's authorized an important legal transaction transforming its unincorporated society to an official nonprofit corporation named St. Peter's Episcopal Church of Oxford, Mississippi, with a perpetual duration and all property duly transferred to the corporation.

St. Peter's Popular Pumpkin Patch

The Rev. Kyle Bennett had begun his three-year tenure as Chaplain in 1994. He soon disbanded the Canterbury Club, the official campus

Episcopalian organization, and expanded St. Peter's outreach to students through a new program, the Episcopal Church at Ole Miss (ECOM). Attendance grew from an average of 20-30 on Sunday evenings to over 100. An innovative mentoring program during this time paired students with parishioners and saw three students off to seminary. Bennett also introduced the popular Pumpkin Patch, which is still funding youth programs in 2011, and creating photographic opportunities for all children in the area. He also introduced disk golf to the community and designed the course at Avent Park in Oxford. The Rev. Charlie Deaton came as Chaplain when the Bennett family moved to the Gulf Coast.

In 1995, the vestry organized a series of home meetings to identify issues that made parishioners happy, concerns they might have, and to hear their suggestions for the future. Over one hundred members participated and the overriding positive comments concerned the warmth of the parish family, the beauty of the sanctuary, and the ministry of The Rev. Duncan Gray, III. People were concerned about the rapid membership growth and the church's ability to keep newcomers connected to the church. By 1996, baptized membership had reached 526: 387 adults and 139 youth under the age of sixteen.

A Spanish Ministry began in 1998. Services continue to be held every Sunday evening under the guidance of The Rev. Deacon Penny Sisson and The Rev. Bruce McMillan of Christ Church, Holly Springs. The first long range planning task force embarked on an extensive procedure to determine St. Peter's greatest needs and reported at the January 23, 2000, annual meeting that space and additional clergy were the areas of greatest need for continued growth of the parish.

In addition to the growth of church membership, the fifteen years under Gray III's leadership were marked by increased community outreach programs and racial reconciliation efforts that were strengthened through programs implemented by Gray and Rev. Leroy Wadlington, Pastor of Second Baptist Church. Young and old alike joined hands in support of these efforts which began with high school students attending a meeting at Second Baptist to discuss ways to begin bridging the gap between the races. Dialogue on bridging racial divide and annual events such as pulpit swaps, congregation swaps, and an annual hymn singing continue to bring the congregations closer to a deeper understanding of one another. The following statement of inclusion was adopted by the Vestry of St. Peter's as requested by Gray after he was named Bishop: *We respect the dignity of all persons, regardless of sexual orientation, national origin, race, gender or age and welcome and encourage them to fully participate in all areas of parish life.*

Gray was named Bishop Coadjutor in 2000 and the third Duncan M. Gray to serve as Bishop of Mississippi in 2003.

Duncan M. Gray, III, 9th Bishop of Mississippi 2003-
Rector at St. Peter's: 1985-2000.

7

Celebrations & Ordinations
2000-2011

St. Peter's had survived the Civil War, vacant pulpits, mission status, two World Wars, the riots of 1962, Vietnam protests, and in the year 2000, was positioned for grand celebrations and historic ordinations in this exciting new century. With the unprecedented growth experienced over the previous ten years, St. Peter's had evolved from a pastoral church structure with the rector as the central leader, into a program church structure, with more leadership coming from the laity. This new structure was designed to encourage more participation from the growing numbers of church members. The Rev. Murray Bullock served as interim rector during the search process for a permanent rector.

The Reverend W. Taylor Moore, Jr. delivered his first sermon at St. Peter's on September 9, 2001, in the midst of a grand celebration of the church's 150-year presence in Oxford. The parish family had kicked off this celebration earlier in January with a candlelight procession from the

Courthouse on the Square, where the first organizational meeting was held in May 1851, to St. Peter's, where they attended a service with music and prayer books from the 1800's. A Homecoming Celebration in May 2001 honored three former rectors who all became Bishops of the Diocese of Mississippi: The Right Rev. Duncan Gray, Jr., The Right Rev. A.C. Marble, and The Right Rev. Duncan M. Gray III. Services honored all clergy who had served at St. Peter's and concluded with the Holy Eucharist and dinner on the grounds. Oral histories of many long-time members were recorded and are preserved in the church's archives. The Rev. Moore had indeed come during a celebratory year. More cause for celebration occurred in 2001 when Penny Sisson was ordained as St. Peter's first Vocational Deacon, also making her the church's first woman clergy.

In October 2002, the Episcopal News Service reported on a public service of Evening Prayer at St. Peter's, when more than 140 people came to commemorate and reflect on the year-long Open Doors observance being held at the University of Mississippi. Retired Bishop Gray, Jr. spoke on campus at a dinner and reminded the audience that "the observance is to focus not so much on what's already been done, but on what still needs to be done." It had been 40 years since the riots of 1962.

The Rev. Deacon Penny Sisson

Pledges surpassed $400,000 in 2002, and many programs were in full swing. Leap Frog served close to 100 children from the first and second grades and had a budget of $50,000 in 2003. Grants, United Way, Oxford-University United Methodist Church, and public contributions helped fund this program begun at St. Peter's in 1989. Ministries to Parchman Penitentiary, the Lafayette County Jail, Haven House, Sunday services at the North Mississippi Regional Center, and services for the Hispanic community continued to contribute to the church's mission. The Honduras Mission was in its twentieth year. More recent ministries now included AMOS, a consortium of churches organized to address quality of life in the local community, and the Ministry with Gay and Lesbian Persons created in 2004 in response to Bishop Gray's call to "…seek out those who are searching but have never been invited in." The election in 2003 of an openly gay bishop in New Hampshire created unrest among some parishioners, and, similar to the turmoil of 1962, a few members cut or restricted pledges. A few left the church. The Rev. Moore, however, received notice in 2006, that St. Peter's ranked 340th out of 7600 missions and parishes in the country in terms of average Sunday attendance. In the Diocese of Mississippi, St. Peter's was the third largest parish in membership and the second largest in average Sunday attendance.

Unlike the atmosphere in 1962, and just one year after the 2002 Open Doors program at the University, St. Peter's welcomed with open arms the first African American priest in its history, The Rev. Ollie Rencher, who would serve as Chaplain for the Episcopal Church at Ole Miss and Assistant Rector for St. Peter's. *The Oxford Eagle's* January 14, 2004 headline story read, "St. Peter's Celebrates Historic Ordination," and noted that The Rev. Rencher was the grandson of one of the last pastors to serve in the original Burns United Methodist Church, now known as the Burns Belfry Building, less than a block away from St. Peter's. Students at the University and parishioners alike responded to this energetic new Chaplain. New outreach programs, such as the Manna Feeding Ministry, thrived under his leadership. ECOM attendance at St. Peter's was at an all time high when Rencher left in 2008 for the Church of the Holy Communion in Memphis.

Ordination of The Rev. Ollie Rencher,
Chaplain/Assistant Rector 2003-2008
Photo courtesy of *The Oxford Eagle*

Historic ordinations at St. Peter's were not over yet. Following The Rev. Rencher as Chaplain was The Rev. Janet P. Oller, who would become the first woman to serve in that official capacity. The Rev. Oller arrived as a Deacon and was ordained to the priesthood in 2010. The Rev. Laura F. Gettys had been serving as Associate Rector since 2007, another historic appointment since she was the first woman priest to serve at St Peter's. Notes from the 1970 General Convention had reported that *in a vote by Orders, defeated ... action that would permit women to be ordained priests and bishops as well as deacons....* The ordination of women to priesthood passed six years later at the 1976 convention and although 200 female deacons had been ordained, there were none in Mississippi. By 2010, St. Peter's had three female clergy and seven female vestry members, one of whom was serving as Senior Warden.

Also in 2010, another 150th Celebration was taking place – this time it was not for the establishment of the church, but the birthday of the actual church building where the first service was held on Easter Sunday in 1860. A yearlong celebration started on Pentecost Sunday with an old fashioned picnic, and like the 125th Celebration in 1976, offered a showing of *Intruder in the Dust* that opened with scenes from St. Peter's and in which The

Rev. William Asger and members of the parish appeared for a few seconds in the 1949 film. As part of this anniversary celebration, the church established an official Archive with volumes of Annual Parish Reports, Vestry Minutes, Newsletters, historical clippings, documents, and hundreds of photographs. Notebooks with these items are now indexed and accessible for researchers working on the next update, the 4th Edition of the History of St. Peter's, surely to follow in 2060. This celebration ended on Youth Sunday 2011, with the youth presenting a time capsule of past and present items and their visions of the future of St. Peter's. The time capsule was placed in the columbarium and will be opened by future generations. Another first took place this day when a young member of the Hispanic Community, Jose Rodriquez, stood behind the pulpit and delivered a moving address to young and old parishioners alike at the morning service.

The next chapter of this current history has been reserved for the land and the building. Having this part of St. Peter's history in its own section allows the story of our sacred space to be told from the beginning to the present day without interruptions from the life inside its historic walls.

The Reverend W. Taylor Moore, Rector 2001-2015

8

The Land and The Building

It was during Frederick A.P. Barnard's tenure as rector that the present building, chancel and nave were erected. The lot had been purchased on November 19, 1855, for $600 from Philip A. and Mary D. Yancey. The following abstract of land deeds reveals transactions for title of the land where St. Peter's stands today. The complete list of transactions is included in the Appendix.

P. A. YANCY: P. A. Yancy and wife, Mary D. Yancy, conveyed the subject property, City Block N, Lots 2 and 3, to the **WARDENS & VESTRY OF THE EPISCOPAL CHURCH AND THEIR SUCCESSORS IN OFFICE** for the sum of Six Hundred Dollars ($600.00) on the 19th day of November 1855.

WARDENS AND VESTRY MEN: On June 26, 1883, the Vestry Men of St. Peter's Episcopal Church conveyed by deed to G. D. Sedgeway, R. R. Bailey, and Marcellus Green, **TRUSTEES OF THE EPISCOPAL FUND**, the west one-half (½) of Block N, Lots 2 and 3, in the Town of Oxford, for the purpose of an Episcopal residence for the Rt. Rev. H. M. Thompson, with the understanding that Bishop H. M. Thompson should make his permanent home in the Town of Oxford. After Bishop Thompson made his home in the City of Jackson, Mississippi, consideration for the conveyance failed.

TRUSTEES OF THE EPISCOPAL FUND: Consideration for the conveyance having failed, the Trustees of the Episcopal Fund reconveyed to P. H. Skipwith, N. B. Pegues, C. W. Sears, J. C. Wheeler, J. A. Jenkins, L. P. Coleman, and C. H. Keyes, **WARDENS AND VESTRY OF ST. PETER'S EPISCOPAL CHURCH, OXFORD, MISSISSIPPI, AND THEIR SUCCESSORS**, the west half of Block N, Lots 2 and 3, on June 9, 1887.

WARDENS AND VESTRY OF ST. PETER'S EPISCOPAL CHURCH: Title to Block N, Lots 2 and 3, remains vested in the **WARDENS AND VESTRY OF ST. PETER'S EPISCOPAL CHURCH**.

This copy of an early photo taken before the spire was added in 1893 was found in church files. This beautiful church is the oldest religious structure in Oxford, having survived the burning of the town during the Civil War.

The structure, built by William Turner, was completed in 1860, and Barnard preached the first sermon in the church on Easter Sunday, April 8, 1860. In his sermon, Barnard congratulated the congregation: *"that you are, at length gathered together in this beautiful, though unpretending edifice reared by yourselves to the worship of God. Hitherto, like the Israelites in their captivity, you have had neither temple nor altar and in...your privation and desolation you have suffered as they suffered, when by the rivers of Babylon, they sat down and wept."*

The 1975 application to the National Register of Historic Places describes the church as architecturally being an example of Early English style of Gothic Revival Church. The application reads: "St. Peter's closely resembles Episcopal churches designed and influenced by Richard Upjohn during the decade of the 1850s. It is likely that the planners of the Oxford church were familiar with Upjohn's *Rural Architecture* (1852). ...many features of St. Peter's church resemble elements repeatedly employed by Upjohn in his design for small churches."

The newly erected church was valued at $10,000, but was not consecrated for eleven years because Canon Law required that a building must be debt-free before consecration. A handwritten record of church events compiled by Mrs. Rebecca (Alexander) Pegues contains this entry: *"The Bishop consecrated this Church at his June 18, 1871 visitation. He says, through the generous contributions of a few friends, (among whom was the builder himself, the only creditor), the debt had just been extinguished, and the building made free to be set apart for God's service."* A copy of her lovely handwritten record, which covers the years 1850 to 1871, is in the church's archives.

Bills and receipts pertaining to labor and materials in the building of St. Peter's reveal this information:

- $1,850.60 paid to J.F. Dunlap for laying 370,120 bricks to construct church (UM Professor E.C. Boynton's original detailed calculations that determined the number of bricks are on file in the church archives).
- $1,000 to Wm. Turner on contract for building Episcopal Church
- $400 to J.D. Grace on contract for building Episcopal Church
- $178.38 to M. Dove for plastering
- 25 barrels of lime and plaster of paris from Stratton & McDavid Co. (Memphis)
- $731 for the altar windows, made by the firm of Henry Sharp of New York, not Belgian craftsmen as was long believed until records appeared showing the New York's firm's work

The baptismal font was given in 1873 in memory of Casper Macon Thompson and the altar cross and vases were given in memory of Thomas E.B. Pegues the following year. The altar rail was given in 1881, but it was 1887 before the altar was put in place and the organ moved from the rear of the church. A more complete list of early gifts and memorials is included in the Appendix.

The exterior of the church was completed in 1890, when in Appendix II of Bishop Thompson's address, he stated, *"the property of St. Peter's Church, Oxford, consisting of ½ a square in the town of Oxford, is vested in Wardens and Vestry of the church."* Mrs. Rebecca Pegues made a gift of the dormered octagonal spire, sheathed with tin stamped in a fish pattern. The church dedicated it to her memory in 1893. Between 1923 and 1927, the chancel was raised, the choir moved and placed between the nave and altar, and the arch-paneled railway to accommodate the pulpit was added.

1949 from church files

The frame rectory, built on the south side of the church in 1882 or 1883 (sources cite both), underwent many transformations and deserves its own space in this building history. It had been converted to office use in 1949. Then, almost 60 years after it was constructed, the rectory was remodeled during the church's centennial year in 1951. Under the leadership of The Rev. William Asger, the building now included a parish house and upstairs apartment. The Right Reverend Duncan M. Gray, Sr. dedicated the new parish house on April 7, 1951. The entire structure was eventually demolished when a new Parish House, consisting of Sunday School rooms, student center, and kitchen was built in 1956-57.

Photo courtesy of Sara Davidson, front of rectory before
demolition, mid-1950s.

The Rev. Emile Joffrion launched an aggressive fundraising campaign with a $75,000 goal in 1956. Church records indicate the price tag was closer to $90,000. In explaining the need for this Parish House, Joffrion wrote in his Building Program brochure:

"Our physical need – the need for a Parish House – is emphatic. ...will serve as a Sunday School for our children, as a meeting place for our Canterbury Club and youth groups. In a University community, it will serve the needs of University groups in our Church in a Christian atmosphere.... It will be a focus of Church service to our community."

1956 Renovation Drawing

Picture from church files identified as "brick from Oxford, England in corner-stone." The Reverend Emile Joffrion and Oxford, MS Mayor Dick Elliott

Five short years after the 1956 expansion, another important addition to the church was the installation of a Pels Organ, made in Alkmaar, Holland. The organ's reeds and blowers came from Germany, England, and Switzerland. The purchase of the organ was made possible by a check for $22,500 from Mrs. Robert M. Carrier and a generous bequest from Miss Kate Skipwith. The organ was used for the first time at services on Sunday, October 15, 1961, and was formally dedicated on November 19 in memory of Mr. Carrier. During this same year, under the leadership of The Rev. Duncan Gray, Jr., St. Peter's underwent the first of a three-stage renovation which included replacing pews, removing an archway, and installing ornamentally screened enclosures to support the organ pipes.

An interesting account of the old manual pump organ was told by John M. Pegues, Jr. in his response to a request for church memories for the sesquicentennial in 2001. Mr. Pegues told how the organist, his great-aunt Lottie White, depended on a manual pump in the basement to provide air to the organ. Mr. Pegues father manned the pumps and would wait on a signal from Miss White to start pumping. When she would get too interested in the sermon to remember to signal, his father had a time getting enough air in the manifold. Mr. Pegues remembered remains of the old pump being in the basement in the late 1940s.

The spire and narthex were renovated during the second phase of renovation, completed in the fall of 1963. The bell tower and steeple were later stabilized during 1992-93 at a cost of approximately $60,000.

The final phase of the 60s work was completed in May 1965, resulting in replastered walls, refinished windows, installed storm windows, and replaced wainscoting. One other alteration of note during the 60s occurred when The Rev. H. M. Morse centralized the altar by moving it away from the east wall. The gold leaf lettering above the side windows was completed in 1969 by Cecil Lantrip. The lettering had been done earlier, possibly in 1883 for an Easter Festival, but this date is undocumented. In the spring of 1974, the bricks were sandblasted, the steeple repaired, and its cross painted gold.

Undated photo by Richard Wilcox, church archives

On Palm Sunday 1995, The Rev. Duncan Gray III blessed the church grounds in preparation for a major redevelopment project, costing more than $500,000, which was completed in 1996. This new southwest wing provided additional Sunday School space and meeting rooms, renovations to the Parish Hall (Student Center), new office space, improvements to the kitchen, and new carpet for the sanctuary.

Corner of 9th St. and Van Buren in 1996

South 9th St. view of 1996 addition

2011
Photo Courtesy of Margaret Wylde

Columbarium 1996
Photo by Brenda West

More recent additions and acquisitions include a columbarium, which was built in 1996 beside the altar, where the sacristy had been. A local craftsman built the drawers and members were given an opportunity to purchase a space for $500. The Vestry voted in 2000 to purchase a new Schantz Pipe Organ, estimated to cost $285,340 plus $15,000 in related expenses. An aggressive campaign to finance the purchase began immediately. In 2001, the church property expanded for the first time with the purchase of a house and lot across from the church at 906 Van Buren.

A chapter on the building would not be complete without documentation of the historical windows. Copies of Jean Kiger's *The Stained Glass Windows of St. Peter's Episcopal Church* are available in the church office. *"The church has been a sanctuary, a refuge from turmoil. These windows have filtered out and transfigured the light from the outside world. They enable us to see visions of the world more as God intended and to act on those visions."*

Moore offers this review on the church website: *"The book features excellent prints of all of the windows in the historic 1860 church building ... Each window has an explanation of the history of the window with information about the donor families where applicable. Other essays include a brief history of the parish, a general essay about the windows and an article on St. Peter's windows by renowned stained glass expert, Virginia Raguin. Charles Reagan Wilson served as the editor; Jean Moore Kiger was the Project Director, benefactor, and the author of the general essay; Langdon Clay was the photographer. The book was published by the Nautilus Publishing Company in 2007."*

2011
Photo Courtesy of Margaret Wylde

2011
Photo Courtesy of Margaret Wylde

9

The New Millennium

Charles Reagan Wilson, in an essay he wrote for the Sesquicentennial celebration in 2001, "St. Peter's Spiritual Autobiography," reminds us *"that our spiritual lives are lived not only as individuals but as members of a spiritual community, St. Peter's, which has left a mark on this place."* He concludes with a passage from Psalm 103: *"As for man, his days are as grass: as a flower of the field, so he flourisheth. For the wind passeth over it and it is gone; and the place thereof shall know it no more."* Wilson reflects that our days here as numbered individuals are not entirely like the grass of the fields. *"Because collectively we have memory and remember the achievements of those like us in the past, those at St. Peter's who once sat and prayed to our God here, and worked here for others, part of the accumulated experience that is our inheritance and will be our legacy to the future."*

The Reverend Janet Oller, Dr. Charles Reagan Wilson, Brenda J. West
placing materials in the columbarium to ensure the preservation of our collective
memories for future generations.

Appendix

Bishops of the Diocese of Mississippi

William Mercer Green	1849- 1887
Hugh Miller Thompson	1883-87 Coadjutor 1887-1902
Theodore DuBose Bratton	1903-1938
William Mercer Green II	1919-1938 Coadjutor 1938-1942
Duncan Montgomery Gray	1943-1966
John Maury Allin	1961-1966 Coadjutor 1966-1974
Duncan M Gray, Jr.	1974-1993
Alfred Clark Marble, Jr.	1991-1993 Coadjutor 1993-2003
Duncan M. Gray, III	2000-2003 Coadjutor 2003-2015
Brian R. Seage	2014 – 2015 Coadjutor 2015 – Present

*The Rt. Rev. James Hervey Otey, provisional Bishop of Mississippi, visited Oxford in 1848: "read morning prayer, baptized three children, and preached." Bishops Journal.

Rectors Who Served St. Peter's Church

Before Frederick A.P. Barnard became the first resident clergyman in 1855, names and dates of those who served as rector are difficult to confirm. Some names in the Diocesan Journal entries transcribed by Miss Frances Walthall differ slightly from Asger's history and *The Episcopal Church in Mississippi*. A few dates from Rebecca Pegues' handwritten journal differ slightly still. Since the Pegues' children were baptized during this time and family members served as lay readers when there was no rector, I have relied heavily on the accuracy of her entries.

All sources agree that The Reverend Chauncey Colton, head of St. Thomas Hall and Christ Church in Holly Springs, made monthly visits to St. Peter's in the early 1850s, and that The Reverend Thomas B. Lawson of Marshall County also visited St. Peter's during this early period. The Reverend Andrew Matthews visit in 1840 is documented in Chapter One.

Frederick A.P. Barnard	1855-1861 1st resident clergyman
Francis A. Shoup	1868 admitted to diaconate; ordained and left 1869
Wallace Carnahan	1871-1872 Dec. '71-Mar.'72
Frederick A. Juny	1872-1875
Stephen H. Green	1875-1877 made monthly visits
James T. Pickett	1878-1881 from Holly Springs; no permanent rector
Melville M. Moore	1883-1884
Edward Lewis	1884-1886 Dean of St. Peter's Pro Cathedral

Rectors Who Served St. Peter's Church

John A. Harris	1886-1892 ordained to diaconate 1886; ordained to priesthood 1887; resigned 1888; returned 1889
Herbert E. Bowers	1893 Deacon
Edmund A. Neville	1899 Missionary; Rector 1900
Clement D. Brown	1903-1916
E. Sterling Gunn	1918-1919
Bradner J. Moore	1923-1927
Edward McCrady	1928-1939
William M. Green, Jr.	1939-1943
Charles S. Liles	1943-1945
William M. Green, Jr.	1945-1948
William Asger	1949-1953
Emile Joffrion	1954-1957
Duncan M. Gray, Jr.	1957-1965
Hugh McDonald "Don" Morse	1965-1974
A.C. Marble, Jr.	1974-1978
J. Douglas Stirling	1978-1985
Duncan M. Gray III	1985-2000
Murray Bullock (Interim)	2000-2001
W. Taylor Moore, Jr.	2001 – 2015
David A. Elliott III (Interim)	2015 – 2016
Jody Burnett	2016 – Present

Associate Rectors, Assistant Rectors/Chaplains, Deacons

ASSOCIATE RECTORS

2007-2010	Laura Gettys
2011 – 2018	Ann Whitaker
2018 – Present	Jennifer Southall

ASSISTANTS/CHAPLAINS

1961-1964	Wofford Smith (Assistant)
1966-1968	William C. Morris (Assistant)
1969-1971	David A. Elliott III (Assistant)
1971-1974	A.C. Marble, Jr. (Assistant)
	Named Bishop of Mississippi, 1993
1975-1977	James McGhee (Assistant)
1979-1982	John-Michael Van Dyck (Chaplain)
1984-1986	Paul E. Stricklin (Chaplain)
1986-1987	Terry Minchow-Proffitt (Chaplain)
1987-1989	Hal T. Hutchison (Chaplain)
1990-1993	John McKee Sloan (Chaplain)
	Named Bishop of Alabama, 2001
1994-1997	Kyle Bennett (Chaplain)
1997-2001	Charles Deaton, Jr. (Chaplain)
2003-2008	Ollie Rencher (Chaplain)
2009-2011	Janet P. Oller (Chaplain)
2011 – 2013	Seth Walley (Chaplain)
2014 – 2018	Chris Robinson (Chaplain)
2019-present	Kirk LaFon

VOCATIONAL DEACONS

2001-present	Penny Sisson

BISHOP IN RESIDENCE

2017 – Present	Duncan M. Gray III

Senior Wardens Who Served

(Early wardens were not always named in journals or diocesan statements. There may have been others who served between 1851 and 1880).

1851	John Millington
1852-1867	Wardens not named
1867–1878	Theo. E.B. Pegues
1878	C. W. Sears
1880-1883	W.B. Pegues
1885-1897	P.H. Skipwith
1898-1911	C.H. Keys
1912-1925	J.E. Pegues
1926-1929	L.E. Thatcher
1930	(No name listed).
1931-1948	Joe Pegues, Jr.
1949 – 1958	W. Ross Brown
1959	C. M. "Tad" Smith
1960-1964	Robert L. Holley
1965	Arthur B. Custy
1966	George Horton
1967	J. Roger McHenry
1968	Michael de L. Landon
1969	M. C. "Chooky" Falkner
1970	H. L. "Ham" Williston
1971	A. Eugene Lee
1972-1973	Michael de L. Landon
1974-1976	J. Roger McHenry
1977	Grady Tollison
1978	Pat Wilson
1979-1980	Michael de L. Landon
1981	Bill Walker
1982	Charles Moseley
1983	Duke Goza
1984	Charles Alexander

Senior Wardens Who Served

1985	Jeanne Holley (1st woman)
1986	Ed Sisson
1987	Ben Banahan
	(filled unexpired term of Chip Davis)
1988	Charles Alexander
1989	Duke Goza
1990	A. Eugene Lee
1991	Wilson Webb
1992	Duke Goza
1993	Lou Zehnder
1994	Ed Sisson
1995-1996	Brenda West
1997	Kathy Knight
1998-1999	Marty Dunbar
2000-2001	Cal Mayo
2002	Ed Sisson
2003	Kaye Bryant
2004	Alan Strand
2005	John Samonds
2006-2007	Dewey Knight
2008	Glen Evans
2009	Herron Rowland
2010	Gloria Kellum
2011-2012	Michael Worthy
2013-2014	Marty Dunbar
2015-2016	John Samonds
2017	Leslie Banahan
2018	Bryon Cohron
2019	Dewey Knight

Early Gifts and Memorials

Alms Basins	From the William Ross Brown family, 1950
Alms Receiving Basin	In Memory of Jimmy Gant
Altar	In Memory of William Mercer Green, 1st Bishop of Mississippi, d1887
Altar Cloth	In Memory of Virginia Moore, d1883
Altar Cross	In Memory of Thomas E. B. Pegues, d1874
Altar Missal	In Memory of Joella Pegues Sheegog
Altar Missal Stand	From Miss Lee H. Randle, Easter 1884
Altar Rail	In Memory of Eliza Tate Hunt d1873; John Thompson d1875; William Hunt Thompson d1881; Casper Wister Thompson d1868
Altar Vases	In Memory of Thomas E. B. Pegues, d1874
American Flag	From Mary Skipwith Buie
Baptismal Font	In Memory of Casper Macon Thompson, d1868
Bible	In Memory of Mable Jenkins Bowen
Bronze Plaque in Parish House	In Memory of Frances Devereux Skipwith, d1884
Candelabra	From Mary Carter Buie and Kate Anderson Skipwith, 1927
Chalice	In Memory of Kate Skipwith's deceased family members, 1939
Chalice	In Memory of Alice Bradford Wilson, d1950
Children's Altar	From Col. Hugh Evans, 1950
Ciborium	In Memory of The Rev. Edward McCrady, Rector 1928-1939
Cruets	In Memory of Joe E. Pegues
Eucharistic Candlesticks	In Memory of Peyton H. Skipwith, and Cornelia Green Skipwith
Hymn Board	From members of Ministering Children's League, 1892
Lanterns	From Mary Skipwith Buie, 1937
Lavabo	From Mrs. David Moore Robinson, 1949
Lectern	From the children of the parish, 1884
Lights	In Memory of Peyton H. Skipwith, John A. Skipwith, Cornelia Green Skipwith
Litany Desk	In Memory of Maria E. Moore, d1873
Paten	In Memory of The Rev. John Augustus Harris. Rector 1886-1892
Pedestals for Eucharistic Candles	In Memory of Elise Pegues

Early Gifts and Memorials

Processional Cross	In Memory of John Adair Skipwith, d1915
Spire	In Memory of Mrs. Alexander (Rebecca) Pegues
White Altar Hangings	From Kate Skipwith, 1950
White Chalice Veil, burse, Pulpit Fall	From St. Catherine's Guild, 1951, made by Mrs. Duncan Whiteside
White Cushion	From Mrs. John Falkner, 1950
Windows	For a complete history of memorial windows, including dates of death, see *The Stained Glass Windows of St. Peter's Episcopal Church*
Window 3	In Memory of Wesley Irving Knight
Window 4	In Memory of Marjorie Vivian Briggs Wallace
Window 5	In Memory of John and Lucille Ramey Falkner
Window 6	In Memory of Dr. Robert Leon Holley, Jr.
Window 7	In Memory of Kirk and Kinard Families
Window 8	In Memory of Samuel Wilds Evans Pegues
Window 9	In Memory of Frances Skipwith & Peyton Horatio Skipwith
Window 10	In Memory of Nicholas and Mary Saunders Pegues
Window 12	In Memory of Peyton Skipwith, Jr., John Adair Skipwith, Frank Polk Skipwith
Window 14	In Memory of Gene Lee (window in parish hall)
Rose Window	In Memory of Henry Talliaferro Buie (window in parish hall)

(Known dates of death are given to memorials.
Dates of gifts are listed when known).

Facts and Legends

■ Once thought to have been designed by famed architect Richard Upjohn who designed Trinity Church in New York, St. Peter's is now accepted as having been influenced, not designed, by this famous architect. It is the oldest religious structure in Oxford.

■ Church legend from the Civil War reports that the church women concealed large quantities of salt in the north wall, hoping to hide it from the invaders. Years later when plaster was applied to the wall, the unforgotten salt absorbed the moisture and caused the plaster to peel. Moisture problems continue to plague the walls today.

■ Notes on an old photo in church archives reads, "Legend has it that one of Grant's cannon balls is (or was) lodged in the steeple as he bombarded the town when advancing down the Memphis Road."

■ *Intruder in the Dust*, based on William Faulkner's novel, was filmed in Oxford in 1949, and has scenes from inside the church building.

■ *Home from the Hill*, filmed in Oxford in the late 50s, opens with a baptism scene being performed by The Rev. Duncan Gray, Jr. in St. Peter's.

■ Excerpts from Bishop Duncan Gray, Jr.'s address at the Faulkner Centennial, September 25, 1997: *"The William Faulkner I knew considered himself a Christian – at least in the broadest sense of that word. He would not have passed any test of theological orthodoxy, nor would he have wanted to; nor did he have close ties with organized religion. However, he did consider himself a member of St. Peter's Church, albeit a rather inactive one, and he thought of the Rector of St. Peter's as his Pastor – or "Padre" as he put it. ...he believed in a God who cared about the world that He had made and about the people in it.... He believed in life after death and he expressed the same to me on more than one occasion."* Bishop Gray closed his remarks with a quote from Dr. Robert Johnson's address to the Faulkner Conference some 20 years earlier: *"Faulkner is for me a witness to the Christian story of sin and redemption. His power seems anchored in that of the Black Christian community.....It is a prescient, unsophisticated faith. As with the powerful singing coming from the black church at the end of Soldier's Pay: 'It was nothing, it was everything.'"*

Facts and Legends

■ Theora Hamblett's paintings of Peter's release from prison came as a gift from the artist during Duncan Gray, Jr.'s tenure as rector. In a letter dated September 8, 1994, Gray tells of Miss Hamblett inviting him to her house to talk about something that was troubling her. She told Gray that her "church or her minister or some group within the church" had accused her of painting idols or encouraging idolatry. "She was obviously disturbed, but I think I was able to reassure her, and we became friends after that," wrote Gray. Miss Hamblett gave The Rev. Gray the Angel which still hangs in the church, and to St. Peter's through Gray, the six vision paintings now hanging in the Parish Hall with the condition that the set (based on Peter's release from prison [Acts 12: 1-7]) not be broken. A bit of unsolved mystery still exists over the numbering of the pieces since there is no number two in this series. Vision paintings rarely left the artist's possession and they were never sold.

Gift of artist, Theora Hamblett, to The Reverend Duncan M. Gray, Jr.
Photo courtesy of Margaret Wylde.

A History of Land Transactions

The following abstract of Lafayette County land deeds was prepared by Diann Walker Coleman and ECOM participant, Chad Benoit, during spring 2010.

UNITED STATES OF AMERICA: The United States of America held the original title to the 640 acres in Section 21, Township 8 South, Range 3 West, upon which St. Peter's Church is situated.

UNITED STATES OF AMERICA: The United States of America executed a patent conveying the 640 acres in Section 21, Township 8 South, Range 3 West to **PRINCESS HO-KA** of the Chickasaw Tribe on June 29, 1842. (Deed Book 103, Page 423 of the Sectional Index).

PRINCESS HO-KA: Princess Ho-Ka conveyed the subject property to **CHISHOLM, MARTIN, AND CRAIG**. (Deed Book A, Land Deeds, Page 125).

CHISHOLM, MARTIN, AND CRAIG: Messrs. Chisholm, Martin, and Craig conveyed the subject property to the **BOARD OF POLICE**.

BOARD OF POLICE: The Board of Police conveyed that portion of Section 21, Township 8 South, Range 3 West, comprising City Block N, Lot 2, to **S. M. CAROTHERS**. (Deed Book B, Page 293).

BOARD OF POLICE: The Board of Police conveyed that portion of Section 21, Township 8 South, Range 3 West, comprising City Block N, Lot 3, to **J. M. CAROTHERS**. (Deed Book C, Page 125).

S. M. CAROTHERS AND WIFE: By succession, Block N, Lots 2 and 3, vested in **S. M. CAROTHERS AND WIFE**, who conveyed the property to **CASSANDRA GLOVER** on February 2, 1846. (Deed Book D, Page 334).

CASSANDRA GLOVER AND WIFE: Cassandra Glover and Wife conveyed the subject property, City Block N, Lots 2 and 3, to **NEILSON AND WENDALL** on April 4, 1846. (Deed Book D, Page 384).

NEILSON AND WENDALL: Messrs. Neilson and Wendall conveyed City Block N, Lots 2 and 3, to **M. J. COOK** in 1850. (Deed Book F, Page 186).

M. J. COOK: M. J. Cook conveyed City Block N, Lots 2 and 3, to **BEN-BURY WALTON** in 1850. (Deed Book F, Page 187).

BENBURY WALTON: Benbury Walton and wife conveyed City Block N, Lots 2 and 3, to **MARY D. YANCY** on January 18, 1853. (Deed Book G, Page 141).

P. A. YANCY: P. A. Yancy and wife, Mary D. Yancy, conveyed the subject property, City Block N, Lots 2 and 3, to the **WARDENS & VESTRY OF THE EPISCOPAL CHURCH AND THEIR SUCCESSORS IN OF-FICE** for the sum of Six Hundred Dollars ($600.00) on the 19th day of November 1855. (Deed Book H, Page 372).

WARDENS AND VESTRY MEN: On June 26, 1883, the Vestry Men of St. Peter's Episcopal Church conveyed by deed to G. D. Sedgeway, R. R. Bailey, and Marcellus Green, **TRUSTEES OF THE EPISCOPAL FUND**, the west one-half (½) of Block N, Lots 2 and 3, in the Town of Oxford, for the purpose of an Episcopal residence for The Rt. Rev. H. M. Thompson, with the understanding that Bishop H. M. Thompson should make his permanent home in the Town of Oxford. After Bishop Thompson made his home in the City of Jackson, Mississippi, consideration for the conveyance failed.

TRUSTEES OF THE EPISCOPAL FUND: Consideration for the conveyance having failed, the Trustees of the Episcopal Fund reconveyed to P. H. Skipwith, N. B. Pegues, C. W. Sears, J. C. Wheeler, J. A. Jenkins, L. P. Coleman, and C. H. Keyes, **WARDENS AND VESTRY OF ST. PETER'S EPISCOPAL CHURCH, OXFORD, MISSISSIPPI, AND THEIR SUCCESSORS**, the west half of Block N, Lots 2 and 3, on June 9, 1887.

WARDENS AND VESTRY OF ST. PETER'S EPISCOPAL CHURCH: Title to Block N, Lots 2 and 3, remains vested in the **WARDENS AND VESTRY OF ST. PETER'S EPISCOPAL CHURCH**.

Notes and Sources

Chapter 1
Our Firm Foundation

Much of the information in this chapter comes from the two earlier histories of St. Peter's. The first, *A History of St. Peter's Episcopal Church, 1851-1951*, was written by The Reverend William Asger, Rector from 1949-1953, on the occasion of the church's centennial in 1951. The most recent, *A Goodly Heritage*, was written by Dr. John Crews, parishioner and Professor Emeritus of English at The University of Mississippi, for the church's 125th celebration in 1976. Copies of both of these documents are housed in the archives of St. Peter's Episcopal Church, Oxford, Mississippi. Parish reports to the Diocese and entries from Bishops' Journals provided important details about the formation of the church. These journals contain entries by The Rev. Andrew Matthews, Provisional Bishop James H. Otey, The Rev. Thomas B. Lawson, The Rev. Chauncey Colton, and The Right Reverend William Mercer Green, first bishop of Mississippi, all of which were included in earlier works by Asger and Crews.

Mrs. Rebecca Pegues, wife of wealthy landowner Alexander Pegues, was an intellectual parishioner whose journal entries provided an intimate look at the desires for a church in Oxford. Copies of her handwritten *Sketch of St. Peter's, 1851-1871* and pages from her personal journal are located in the church archives.

For a more intimate look at Barnard's life, the reader will find Dr. Allen Cabaniss' *The University of Mississippi, Its First Hundred Years* (1971), and Dr. David Sansing's *The University of Mississippi, A Sesquicentennial History* (1999), to be excellent sources for Barnard's role in the church and the University. Copies of Barnard's early sermons are preserved in the church archives.

Online resources for additional information are cited for those interested in further research. One of the most interesting, Barnard's memoirs, is now easily accessible at:
http://www.archive.org/stream/cu31924031759156/cu31924031759156_djvu.txt (Memoirs of Frederick A.P. Barnard, John Fulton, Columbia University Press, 1896).

Chapter 2
The Civil War Takes Its Toll

The proceedings from the 35th Annual Convention of the Protestant Episcopal Church of the Dicocese of Mississippi, held in Christ Church, Holly Springs, April 25, 26, and 27, 1861, were taken from: *http://docsouth.unc.edu/imls/protestant/protestant.html*.

The convention's publication, *Journal of the Thirty-Fifth Annual Convention of the Protestant Episcopal Church, in the Diocese of Mississippi*, is made available by the Rare Book Collection, University of North Carolina at Chapel Hill. © This work is the property of the University of North Carolina at Chapel Hill. It may be used freely by individuals for research, teaching and personal use as long as this statement of availability is included in the text.

Proceedings of Protestant Episcopal Church in the Confederate States, July 3, 1861, were also made available by the Rare Book Collection, University of North Carolina at Chapel Hill:
http://docsouth.unc.edu/imls/protestant1/menu.html

Details from the 1862 meeting of the General Council of the Protestant Episcopal Church in the Confederate States were found in Duke University's Rare Books collection's online site:
http://www.archive.org/stream/journalofprocee00prot#page/n11/mode/2up.

The Episcopal Church in Mississippi: 1763-1992, published in 1992 by the Episcopal Diocese of Mississippi, offers historical research for those wanting more information on the history of the Diocese. Readers should be aware, however, of multiple errors in the clergy list for St. Peter's on page 342. Using journal entries and material in the church's archive, the list has been corrected to the best of the author's ability and is included in the appendix of this publication. An examination of the Holy Catholic Church after the Civil War is documented in the chapter on Bishop Green.

Rebecca Pegues' entries from her *Civil War Diary, 1860-1866*, show an intelligent and informed, but troubled and frightened woman. Copies of these diary entries and her *Sketch of St. Peter's* are in the church's archives. The author did not locate the original diaries. The photograph of Mrs. Pegues used in this manuscript was copied from Don Doyle's, *Faulkner's County: The Historical Roots of Yoknapatawpha*, 2001.

David Sansing's *The University of Mississippi, A Sesquicentennial History* again provides thoughtful insight on Chancellor Barnard, the man, his sensitivities, his friendship with the Pegues family, and Barnard's tenure at St. Peter's. Sansing also delves into Barnard's friendship with Gen. Sherman and his extensive citations in Chapter Five, "Students and Soldiers," give the reader a wealth of information for additional reading on this critical time of our history.

The photographs of Oxford's devastation and the Courthouse with Federal troops camped on the lawn are copied from Jack Lamar Mayfield's *Images of America: Oxford and Ole Miss*, published in 2009, on behalf of the Oxford-Lafayette County Heritage Foundation. Many of the photographs in this book were collected by the late Patricia Brown Young, whose family has played important roles in the life of St. Peter's from its early days. The Rev. Taylor Moore spoke of her passion for the church and her commitment to racial reconciliation at her burial on May 8, 2007. A copy of this homily is on file in the church office.

John Sobotka's *History of Lafayette County, Mississippi* (1976) was helpful in understanding the devastation of Oxford in 1864.

An early typed document from Miss Frances Walthall provided important documentation from early diocesan journals. What appears to be her signature is followed by: *FROM THE DIOCESAN JOURNALS FOR THE FOLLOWING DATES*. The first entry is dated 1851 and the last is 1924. Efforts to identify Miss Walthall have not produced her connection to St. Peter's. This document is in the church archives.

Chapter 3
Post-War Years

Dr. Cabaniss' *The University of Mississippi, Its First Hundred Years* again supplies us with historical information concerning the close relationship between the University and St. Peter's. Many of the officers returning from the war were connected not only to the University, but also to St. Peter's through various leadership positions.

For details on General Shoup's resignation from the University, thereby leaving St. Peter's once again with a vacant pulpit, see Dr. Sansing's *Sesquicentennial History*, cited earlier.

The legal document giving the vestry authority for the cemetery may be found in the Lafayette County Deed Book N, page 389. Jean Kiger's extensive research is an excellent resource for additional information on the complex arrangement between the city and the church. A copy of her work, *A History of St. Peter's Cemetery*, published in 2008, is available in the church archives and in the Skipwith Room at the Oxford Public Library.

More information on Bishop Thompson's efforts to create worship opportunities for black Mississippians may be found in *The Episcopal Church in Mississippi*, pages 56-58, and 61-63. Additional information on Bishop Green's final years is also included in this history. The Rev. William Asger's centennial history is cited once again in this section.

Chapter 4
1st Half of a New Century

Reference to Mr. Keys' memorial service is found in Asger's 1951 history.

Dr. Cabaniss discusses the University's policy on leaves of absences for World War I service in his history. He also describes the political climate of the University during the Great Depression. So much of what he writes shows a direct impact on parish life at St. Peter's.

The 1899 Record Book of St. Peter's is protected in the bank lock box. It contains this vivid description of the state of the church when Moore arrived in 1923.

A mission is defined as a congregation that is dependent upon the diocese or another "mother" congregation for financial support.

The Episcopal Church in Mississippi: 1763-1992 gives a detailed account of the formation of Camp Bratton Green and the role St. Peter's has played since its beginning.

Bishop Gray's address at the 1997 Faulkner Centennial is on file in St. Peter's archives.

Published proceedings from Diocesan Councils, from the early formation of St. Peter's to current council meetings, provide rich documentation for a better understanding of the Episcopal presence in Mississippi. The 120th Council in 1947 addressed the changes in college ministry and the need for campus ministry for Negroes. Apparently there was no suggestion that this would be anything but a separate ministry in the historically black schools mentioned.

The 1952 council proceedings introduced to the diocese the need for a rectory in Oxford. The first Bishop Gray gave his thoughts on Diocesan support for the rectory since St. Peter's served growing numbers of University students and faculty. He continued his request for support at the next council meeting in 1953.

Proceedings from these meetings again provide important documentation for this manuscript.

The McCrady Scrapbook, compiled by the McCrady family, was located at the University Museums in 2010, after years of not knowing its whereabouts. Copies of the contents are now in Volume 14 in the church archives and the original book is housed in Special Collections at the University of Mississippi Library.

Charles Eagles' article detailing Joffrion's stand when the University denied Rev. Kershaw the right to speak on campus may be accessed at: *http://www.thefreelibrary.com/The+Closing+of+Mississippi+Society:+Will+Campbell,+The+$64,000...-a075085028.*

Joffrion's support of Morton King is documented in special collection at The University of Mississippi:
www.olemiss.edu/depts/general_library/archives/finding_aids/MUM00578.html.

Chapter 5
The Turbulent 60s & 70s

Facts and figures on membership and budgetary matters were all taken from vestry minutes and reports on file in the church office. Of special note was the April 1966 report from the worship evaluating committee and the October 1967 discussion concerning reverting to mission status. The January 1971 minutes showed a budget of $26,801. This reflected the withdrawal of a few pledges over the controversial peace services.

Bishop Gray's sermons of September 30, and October 7, 1962, are housed in the church archives.

Dr. Charles Wilson's complete interview with Bishop Gray, Jr., produced and directed by the University of Mississippi Media and Documentary Projects in 2009, is available online at *http://www.vimeo.com/8036747*.

The telegram from the National Church Council cited is on file in the church archives. The press releases from the Council are found in the Episcopal Church Archives at *http://www.episcopalarchives.org/*. These releases give a good indication of issues our vestry wrestled with in 1969.

Oxford resident Will Lewis donated Kate Skipwith's papers to this project and those relevant to St. Peter's are now in the church archives. These include her will and the final settlement papers. Mr. Lewis also gave St. Peter's a small prayer book that Ms. Skipwith had given his mother.

Will D. Campbell's powerful story about Duncan M. Gray, Jr., published in 1997, is a must read for anyone wanting a personal glimpse into Gray's life and his impact on racial reconciliation efforts. Campbell weaves the story of the University Grays, the CSA regiment made up of University of Mississippi students, into this personal story of his friend: *And Also With You: Duncan Gray and the American Dilemma*.

Araminta Stone Johnston's biography of Duncan M. Gray, Jr., was released in 2011. Johnston grew up in Oxford and her book, *And One Was a Priest*, like Campbell's, tells the powerful story of this courageous man's tenure at St. Peter's during the integration of the University.

Chapter 6
Another Century Winds Down

All of the documentation for this period came from vestry minutes, parish newsletters, and Parish Annual Reports, all of which are on file in the church archives.

Clippings from *The Oxford Eagle* are on file in multiple volumes in the church archives. These may be readily accessed with a search by topic from the computerized index in the church office.

Chapter 7
Celebrations & Ordinations

As in the previous chapter, documentation for this period came from church files, vestry minutes, monthly newsletters, and Annual Parish Reports. Church Archives also contain volumes of indexed material available to those wanting to read more about this period. Volume 13 contains official programs from ordinations of many who served as chaplains or rectors at St. Peter's.

Chapter 8
The Land & the Building

The abstract of land deeds was prepared with information on file in the Lafayette County Chancery Court Clerk Office (Deed Book H).

Documentation on the building from its original construction in 1860, to the last renovation, is all located in the church archives. Of special interest are Professor Boynton's handwritten calculations in Volume 9 on the number of bricks needed to build the church.

The Stained Glass Windows of St. Peter's Episcopal Church, Oxford, Mississippi, published in 2007 by Nautilus Publishing Company, provides detailed information on the windows and a brief history of the families represented by them. Charles Reagan Wilson was editor and Jean Kiger was Project Director. Copies of this beautiful publication, with color photographs by Langdon Clay, are available in the church office.

Other important information for this chapter was taken from the National Historic Site application forms, submitted by Lisa Reynolds for the Mississippi Department of Archives and History in April 1975. These forms are filed in Volume 1 in the church archives.

Chapter 9
The New Millennium

Professor Charles Reagan Wilson's essay is a part of the 2001 sesquicentennial papers, filed in Volume 30 of church archives. The time capsule was placed in the church columbarium to be enjoyed by future generations. A list of the contents is filed in Volume 31 of church archives.

The Appendix

Lists of bishops, rectors, associate rectors, assistant rectors, chaplains, and senior wardens were verified to the best of the author's ability. Discrepancies were noted in both church files and in *The Episcopal Church in Mississippi*.

The Rev. Duncan M. Gray Jr.'s letter explaining Theora Hamblett's gift of her vision paintings is filed in Volume 16 in the church archives. The artist's 1975 publication, *Theora Hamblett Paintings*, in collaboration with Ed Meek and William S. Haynie, contains a similar set with a full description of Peter's release from prison. This book also contains many earlier paintings, as well as numerous biblical scenes.

About the Author

A native of Hopkinsville, Kentucky, Brenda Jones West has lived in Oxford since 1973 when her husband Bill was assigned to teach ROTC at the University of Mississippi. The mother of two daughters, Michele and Debby, she left her church and followed them to St. Peter's where they had become involved in EYC. The entire family was soon confirmed by Bishop Gray, Jr., and all became active members of the growing Episcopal community. She earned two degrees from the University before she began her professional career with the Ole Miss Alumni Association. She served as Senior Warden two years with Bishop Duncan Gray III. Now retired, she has had the joy of seeing all three grandchildren baptized at St. Peter's.

Almighty God, We give you thanks for the fellowship of those who have worshipped in the place, and we pray that all who seek you here may find you, and be filled with your joy and peace; through Jesus Christ our Lord, who lives and reigns with you, in the unity of the Holy Spirit, one God, now and forever. *Amen.*

(Contemporary Collect #2, *Book of Common Prayer, 1979, p.254*)

Eternal God, the heaven of heavens cannot contain you, much less the walls of temples made with hands. Graciously receive our thanks for this place, and accept the work of our hands, offered to your honor and glory. For this place where we may be still and know that you are God, We thank you, Lord.

(A Litany of Thanksgiving for a Church, *Book of Common Prayer, 1979, p.578*)

Notes

Notes